Quar. Rev. of Film & Video, Vol. 11, pp. i
Reprints available directly from the publisher
Photocopying permitted by license only

Harwood Academic Publishers, 1989
Printed in the United States of America

A Note to Our Readers

The Editors and Publisher are pleased to present this first issue in a new format with a new title. The *Quarterly Review of Film Studies* has become the *Quarterly Review of Film and Video* and is now published by Harwood Academic Publishers.

As our friends and contributors know, the journal over the last two years has fallen considerably behind because of delays by the former publisher. We have now published two issues with Harwood, and the remaining back-logged material will appear in the near future. In addition to general issues dealing with a wide range of topics in film and television studies, special issues now in preparation include *Film Parody*, edited by Ronald Gottesman; *Indian Popular Cinema*, edited by Mira Binford; and *Phenomenology and Cinema*, edited by Frank Tomasulo.

Along with a new publisher comes a new name, focus, and direction. To reflect the growing attention accorded to study of television and video by film scholars around the world, we have added the word *Video* to the title. The term designates the electronic medium in the broadest terms, encompassing the study of broadcast television and artists' video as well as emerging technologies. A statement of the journal's new Aims and Scopes is included on the inside front cover of this issue.

The journal is also under new editorial direction. While Ronald Gottesman will remain involved as Executive Editor, Katherine S. Kovacs has assumed the position of Editor-in-Chief. In addition, Michael Renov is now the Associate Editor and Mark Williams is the Managing Editor. A number of new members have joined the Editorial and Advisory Boards and additional appointments are pending.

We are excited by the changes taking place and we look forward to offering again an important scholarly forum for the film and video communities. We invite your continued support.

Katherine S. Kovacs

Quar. Rev. of Film & Video, Vol. 11, pp. iii–vi
Reprints available directly from the publisher
Photocopying permitted by license only

Harwood Academic Publishers, 1989
Printed in the United States of America

BEVERLE ANN HOUSTON (1935–1988)

A Tribute by Marsha Kinder read at a Memorial Event on May 4, 1988 at the USC School of Cinema-Television for the Dedication of the Beverle Houston Critical Studies Seminar Room and the establishment of the Beverle Houston Scholarship Fund. In addition to other speakers, the event also included the screening of an excerpt featuring Beverle Houston from "Soft Fiction" (1979) by Chick Strand and a 29-minute video tribute by Bruce Yonemoto, Patty Podesta and Norman Yonemoto called "Pleasure: Impressions of Beverle Houston's Critical Writings."

Beverle Ann Schwartzman was born in West Reading, Pennsylvania on December 23, 1935, and grew up in Philadelphia. When her parents separated, Beverle and her mother Jeanne moved in with her aunt and uncle and their two children Bede and Joey. So she grew up in an extended family, which was a very important fact in Beverle's life. Beverle was never very rebellious against her family; she always felt a strong solidarity with them. She expected women to be strong and independent like her mother and aunt, whether single or married. And that experience helped Beverle's feminism come more naturally to her.

When Beverle was in the fourth grade, her teacher informed the class that children from broken homes are unhappy and should be pitied. Beverle immediately stood up and told the teacher that that was not true—that her parents were divorced and yet *she* was still a happy child living in a happy home and certainly didn't need to be pitied. Beverle was sent to the principal's office for being rude and for contradicting the teacher, but she immediately became a mythic figure for her classmates. What this story so vividly reveals about Beverle is, not only her moral courage and indomitable spirit, but also her fierce loyalty to her mother and to the rest of her extended family. And also an absolute confidence in her own emotional reality.

Though Beverle had many remarkable strengths—physical, intellectual, spiritual and verbal—it was her emotional honesty that was perhaps the most remarkable of all. When you were with Beverle you were always confronted with her emotional honesty, which forced *you* to be more honest yourself—whether you were a relative, a friend, a husband, a lover, a student, a colleague, an acquaintance, a committee, or an institution. And that made you feel more like extended family.

For Beverle, being raised in an extended family could never be a handicap; she saw it as desirable. She used to fantasize that some day she and all of her close friends would retire and live together in one big happy family. Although she may not have lived long enough to fulfill that fantasy, all through her life she was drawn toward extended families and helped to create them around her.

While Beverle was an undergraduate at the University of Texas (a double major in English and Journalism), she decided to get a summer job at Grossingers, the most well known resort hotel in the Catskills. Not only did she demonstrate her extraordinary intelligence and dazzling administrative abilities by quickly being promoted to a position at the front desk, but she also won the heart of one of the Grossinger heirs. They were married at the resort and had room service ever after, and Beverle became a member of one of the most legendary extended families in America. Although such a fairy tale marriage might be the dream of many a Jewish American Princess, for Beverle it soon turned into Rapunzel. She walked away from the marriage and the money and went to Graduate School at the University of Pennsylvania where she would get her M.A. in English literature and where she would meet her second husband David Houston.

David was the total antithesis of the Grossingers—very blond and Anglo-Saxon, a Marxist economics professor who refused to own property but who also saw himself as a Hemingway hero. They toured through Europe on a motor bike and then came to UCLA where David had a new job and Beverle entered the doctoral program in English literature. It was 1962, and that's when Beverle and I became friends.

What immediately struck me about Beverle was how much fun it was to be with her, no matter what you were doing. What a great sense of humor she had, what a capacity for combining shrewdness, wit, idealism, and pleasure. She loved to dance, party, sing, ride horses, cook, and she especially loved to eat and to talk.

Beverle took a sensual pleasure in using words with precision, playfulness and passion—in feeling them roll off her tongue, in hearing their rhythms, and in seeing them take shape on a page. Everyone who knew her has absorbed many of her wonderful expressions. We can hear her voice in our own speech. It winds through our hearts and minds like a bright-colored ribbon. The pleasure that she took in language was part of her extraordinary capacity to relish life in all of its lushness—from the most mundane creature comforts to the most esoteric abstractions.

Together with Rosalie Newell, Beverle and I formed another extended family at UCLA—like the proverbial three sisters, all studying 18th century English literature under Ralph Cohen, whom we considered the most brilliant professor at the University and who became our intellectual father. Our husbands and our fellow students used to tease us, calling us the formidable female troika as we marched through the halls of the Humanities building three abreast; others called us the Marx sisters. But we felt a great sense of solidarity—in helping each other survive the traumatic jolts of the 60s and in helping each other get our degrees and divorces.

Beverle's dissertation was on Jonathan Swift's *Tale of a Tub* and Laurence Sterne's *Tristram Shandy,* a project that helped to develop her exquisite sense of irony. Her first academic job was in the English Department at Cal State/Northridge, where she proved to be a wonderful, charismatic teacher. In 1968 she was one of the few professors arrested along with students at a political demonstration on behalf of minority rights and, as a consequence, she lost her job and became a cause celebre.

That year there were no openings in 18th century English literature at the local colleges, so Beverle took a job teaching at Oakwood, a private high school in the valley, and the kids were crazy about her. She became totally involved in the life of the school and made a number of lifelong friendships both with her students and their parents. When she returned to college teaching, Oakwood made her a member of their Board of Trustees.

Though she was offered a good job in Canada, Beverle decided to stay in LA, not only because she didn't want to leave her extended family of friends, but also because LA was her favorite city in the world, the capital of post-modernism. So in 1970 she took a job at Pitzer College, where again she was enormously successful as a teacher and as a leader of the faculty.

It was right around this period that Beverle and I were collaborating on our first book, *Close Up*. We started writing together back in 1968. One night we went to see Polanski's *Rosemary's Baby* and both loved it. Then we went to her house for a cup of tea, continuing our heated discussion about what made the film so fascinating. I suggested we write an essay, so we stayed up all night writing, each taking a turn at the typewriter and the other talking away. And when the morning came, the essay was done and we sent it off to *Sight and Sound* where it was published. Together we wrote two books, two screenplays (one on *Tristram Shandy* and the other on *Mary Wollstonecraft*), and twelve articles. And the writing was always enormously enjoyable because there was constant feedback and always lots of laughs. We each absorbed part of the other's style. Beverle was wonderful at choosing precisely the right word or phrase to describe the textures of the image, and I was always obsessed with structure. Even now when I'm writing alone, I sometimes write a sentence that sounds just like Beverle. We both internalized the voice of the other. That's what happens when you write with someone for over ten years.

The last stage of our collaboration was here at USC, in helping to make our Critical Studies Program one of the best in the country. When Beverle applied for the position of Director of Critical Studies, she gave a dazzling presentation called "An Old New Critic Looks at the New Discourse." It was not only brilliant, but also accessible and funny. It honestly reflected her own experience—of having been trained as a humanist in a discourse that prized geniuses and masterpieces, and then having taught herself a new set of theoretical ideas that erased the boundaries between high art and pop culture. These ideas weren't merely abstract concepts for Beverle; they deeply affected her life. They helped her decide to leave Pitzer, to change her primary academic field from literature to film and then to television, to leave her old triumphs behind and to take on new risks. These changes cost Beverle a great deal. She internalized these struggles and even got pneumonia. But they also enabled her to get the job at USC.

Beverle did an extraordinary job as the Director of Critical Studies—as one who demonstrated remarkable abilities as an administrator, who could see the large picture and still attend to the finest details, who had unique intuitive abilities in assessing character and in successfully dealing with a wide range of people, who could make and implement executive decisions while still making us all feel like valued members of an extended family, who immediately elevated the stature of our program, not only within our own School of Cinema-Television, but also within the University at large and within the international field of film and television studies. She knew how to use power; she didn't fear or abuse it.

And while she was devoting all of this energy to administration, she was also making tremendous personal growth as a scholar, in writing her very best work: on the power baby at the center of films by Orson Welles, on Dorothy Arzner's unique methods of subversion, on the metapsychology of television as a medium of endless consumption, on the interaction between television and cinema in defining different spectator positions and different kinds of pleasure. All of these essays drew on and were tested against her own lived experience as an oral personality, as an ardent admirer of melodrama, and as an obsessive consumer of television. They proved to be tremendously influential in the field.

During this same period she also became the co-editor of *Quarterly Review of Film Studies* and helped it to become the best theoretical film journal in the country, generously giving her time to edit the work of other scholars. Beverle was a brilliant editor, a talent which was first demonstrated to the world in her special issue on "Feminist Theory" which she guest edited for *QRFS* in 1978 and which became one of the journal's most influential volumes. I remember in particular how closely she worked with Christine Gledhill on her historic essay, "Recent Developments in Feminist Criticism." And Christine will never forget it either—that's one of the reasons why she has dedicated her latest book on melodrama to Beverle.

During this same period, Beverle was also giving papers at international conferences in London and Urbino, and in the summer of 1984 she was one of the first American film scholars to be invited by the Association of Chinese Film Artists to lecture in China and to have her lectures published in Chinese. She was deeply moved by the Chinese people, by their collective idealism, partly because it appealed so directly to her own feelings about extended family. A wonderful letter from two of her Chinese students, Bao Yuheng and Chen Xihe, clearly demonstrates that she was able to communicate these feelings across the barriers of language and culture. She became their "dear Dr. Beverle" whom they saw as one of the first Americans to encourage their young artists and, as Nick Browne has observed, the first to use the study of melodrama as a means of strengthening the emotional bond between the two cultures.

While Beverle was performing these administrative and scholarly feats at home and abroad, she was also continuing to excel in the classroom here at USC—in developing experimental new courses, in recruiting and supervising some of the best graduate students in critical studies we have ever had, and also in encouraging and supporting some of the most talented students in production.

In all of these ways, Beverle made a tremendous contribution to our School of Cinema-Television and to our field—generously devoting her time, energy, passion and intelligence to this increasingly large extended family. And yet, amazingly, this extraordinary period of accomplishment lasted only four years, from 1982–1986. Beverle felt that these four years as Director of Critical Studies at USC brought her something of great importance in return. She used to tell me that for the first time in her life, she felt she was in a position that demanded her full strength, that enabled her to draw on her full powers. And that was truly exhilarating to Beverle Ann Houston, our "dear Dr. Beverle" who, as the Chinese say, will always share in our victories and always live in our hearts.

Quar. Rev. of Film & Video, Vol. 11, pp. vii–viii
Reprints available directly from the publisher
Photocopying permitted by license only

Harwood Academic Publishers, 1989
Printed in the United States of America

Preface

Female Representation and Consumer Culture

In this issue, *Quarterly Review of Film and Video* renews its concern for the expansion of the critical horizons of film and television scholarship,* examining the filmic text in its relation to a broad range of historical and institutional contexts. "Female Representation and Consumer Culture" adopts a "cultural studies" orientation, an approach to the analysis of popular culture originally and most fruitfully explored in the work of the British Centre for Contemporary Cultural Studies in Birmingham. The object of study from this perspective is the shape, character, and function of all cultural production with cinema considered as one of many symbolic systems. Since the goal of cultural studies is a more complex understanding of contemporary capitalist society and the position of representational forms within that social system, analysis neither begins nor ends with the interpretation of a single text. The cultural studies perspective also shares the political commitment of feminism as Michael Renov demonstrates in his analysis of the ideological function of the image of woman in the U.S. during World War II and its aftermath. Looking at a triad of "mutually reinforcing modalities"—advertising, photojournalism, and cinema—his essay introduces a method for seeing the cinematic image as bolstered by a range of representational enterprises. Other authors take up this interest, examining the allied systems of fashion merchandising and product design and exploring the relationship between shifts in the female image and historical imperatives in the thirties and fifties.

At the center of this issue is the female as consumer of products and fantasies.

Feminist film theory has been concerned for well over a decade with the paradox of the woman/commodity relation; more recently, our comprehension of this diad has been refined and developed through a more theoretically precise formulation of the woman as consumer. Mary Ann Doane in "The Economy of Desire" identifies the essential tautology of the woman's role as consumer which makes her the "subject of a transaction in which her own commodification is ultimately the object."

Like Doane, Jane Gaines on "The Queen Christina Tie-Ups" finds an analogy between the manufacture of cinema and the work of other culture industries which were often harnessed to the promotion of motion pictures in the thirties and forties. By the fifties, as Mary Beth Haralovich finds in "Sitcoms and Suburbs," the product/narrative correspondence constructed an entire social vision as television and suburban architecture and design "created a gender-specific domestic space." With their interest in subcultures as resisting knots or targeted groups, the last two essays illustrate the possibilities of reception theory in the analysis of contemporary mass culture, leading into Lynn Spigel's review of the most recent elaborations of that

---

*See the recent special number, "Television/Film: Cultural Perspectives On History and Theory," 9:3.

methodology—Robert C. Allen's *Speaking of Soaps* and Janice Radway's *Reading the Romance*.

Lynn Spigel and Denise Mann's bibliography, consistent with our cultural studies approach, places cinema in its relation to other forms of mass culture. Here, magazine and television advertising find their place together, with soap opera and women's mass-produced literature considered equally co-terminus, a logic which has been previously demonstrated in Tania Modleski's *Loving With a Vengeance*, reviewed here by Jeanne Allen. Denise Mann's review of Maureen Honey's *Creating Rosie the Riveter*, a comparison of *True Story* magazine and *The Saturday Evening Post* as they were addressed to and received by working class and middle class female readers respectively, raises important issues about the class position of the consuming subject. Giuliana Muscio discusses Marxism as methodology in Stuart and Elizabeth Ewen's *Channels of Desire*, and the semiotic analysis of culture in Judith Williamson's *Decoding Advertisements*, demonstrating the great diversity of recent work on promotional imagery while suggesting its promise for the continuing examination of the woman-as-consumer paradigm.

In this special issue, we offer demonstration of magazines, popular fiction, advertising, and consumer product design as the missing mass cultural links between the culturally hegemonic forms—films and television—on the one hand, and the empirical subject—the consuming woman—on the other. The historical and theoretical inquiries contained in the following pages share a concern for illuminating the relations between disparate, frequently overlapping representational forms and the formation of a specifically female social subjectivity whose political and psychological dimensions far outstrip the economic, consumerist function. It is our view that the expansion of the notion of filmic intertextuality evidenced here can facilitate a more precise and exhaustive account of the network of cultural determinations within which film, television and all its cognate forms are produced and experienced.

Jane Gaines
Michael Renov

Editor's Note: In order to speed up the publication process, the contributors have at our request refrained from making extensive revisions that would have included references to material published since they submitted their articles.

Quar. Rev. of Film & Video, Vol. 11, pp. 1–21
Reprints available directly from the publisher
Photocopying permitted by license only

Harwood Academic Publishers, 1989
Printed in the United States of America

Advertising/Photojournalism/Cinema: The Shifting Rhetoric of Forties Female Representation

Michael Renov

In the opening pages of *Captains of Consciousness*, Stuart Ewen's absorbing study of the development of advertising and its corporate adoption as a tool for social control, an early and unabashed spokesman for the emergent advertising industry is quoted at length. Writing in 1922, Herbert W. Hess describes the intent of advertising's industrial practices as nothing less than the "nullification" of the "customs of ages," the breaking down of "the barriers of individual habits." Like a latter-day Shiva, advertising is, in Hess's words, "at once the destroyer and creator in the process of the ever-evolving new"; its mission—"to superimpose new conceptions of individual attainment and community desire."[1] Ewen's account of advertising's inroads into America's cultural and psychic orientation focuses on the twenties, a decade of dramatic industrial expansion and cultural redefinition; the book's search for the roots of the consumer culture and its deadly serious survey of a broad range of primary sources mark it as a prototypical left exposé. Ewen's work is flawed, however, by its determinist tendencies born of an inadequate theory of ideology, one which abjures components of the unconscious or imaginary in favor of conscious conspiracy theories or, at best, suggestions of "false consciousness." Its limitations notwithstanding, *Captains of Consciousness* is a valuable contribution to the study of American popular culture, laying the groundwork for inquiries into the ensuing permutations of the advertising instinct in American life.

My own work here takes up similar considerations in the analysis of forties female representation and the broad cultural context within which all images of that period were generated. For, indeed, Ewen's claim for the centrality of advertising as a strategy crucial to the corporate construction of social life in America during the twenties finds further illustration two decades later. The advertising motive was, without question, the keystone of cultural production during the war years; the complex and contested body of ideas and images we call ideology in the Althusserian sense was at that moment the object of a remarkable degree of calculation and social engineering in ways to be explored at length. In my own efforts to delimit the forces that constituted the female "vraisemblable" of a decade of Hollywood films, I have borrowed Raymond Williams' definition of ideological

MICHAEL RENOV *is Associate Professor in the School of Cinema-Television at the University of Southern California, Los Angeles, California 90089. He is the author of* Hollywood's Wartime Woman: Representation and Ideology, *UMI Research Press, 1988.*

determination as the elaboration of the pressures and limits within which cultural production occurs.[2]

The search for the roots of the dramatic shifts of forties filmic representation—from Rosie to Gilda and beyond—is gravely impoverished by a blindered approach which defines intertextual space as an ensemble of purely filmic elements, for instance, the other films of a star, director, studio, or year. The cinema has never existed in a representational vacuum; the resonances and overlaps across image domains, as from cinema to advertising imagery to photojournalism, are so many nodal points, markers of ideological veins to be mined.

At stake is a more precisely articulated notion of the way in which a textual regime (a body of woman-centered film texts of a particular historical moment—the forties) comes to be inserted within a dominant ideological formation. Such a project might well consider the work of Terry Eagleton who, in *Criticism & Ideology*, posits a more or less vertical hierarchy of categories for the construction of a materialist criticism of literature, charting an itinerary for the critic which moves from a General to a Literary Mode of Production through a series of ideological strata ("General," "Authorial," and "Aesthetic") before arriving at the text.[3] The contribution of such a schema—despite one's sense of the danger of erecting an idealist topography of the "base/superstructure" variety—is to specify the constituent elements of aesthetic production as "material practice." My own intent here is to expand the analysis of the filmic along a more or less horizontal axis (Mode of Cultural Production) in order to consider coexistent domains of representation. For it is through the consideration of these mutually reinforcing modalities (film, advertising imagery, and photojournalism) that the critic can move toward the interpretive goal suggested by Roland Barthes in *S/Z* ("To interpret a text is not to give it a meaning, but on the contrary to appreciate what plural constitutes it").[4] The braid of voices internal to the text which Barthes elucidated in that work could never be wholly contained or sealed off; the cultural or referential code in particular was envisioned as "a perspective of quotations."[5] The object of this study is to further illuminate that horizon of parallel cultural practices that sustained and animated the woman-centered cinema of the forties, to pay renewed attention to those "off-stage voices" that can be heard alongside all cultural utterance.[6]

Yet another argument for the value of the intertextual as critical focus is provided by Marx's most fundamental remarks on the nature of the commodity in *Capital*. The coextensive cultural forms at issue here may be distinguished by their specific *qualities* (as use-values), but as exchange-values they are merely different *quantities* expressed through a shared representational currency contained within the hegemonic. If Marx argued that "a commodity can acquire a general expression of its value only by all other commodities, simultaneously with it, expressing their values in the same equivalent,"[7] one might equally say that the represented female, situated within and across various image domains, can only be evaluated within an expanded constellation of equivalent forms. For the commodification of the woman effects a kind of levelling to which the present concerns for the "horizontal" or intertextual axis of forties female representation responds. The commodified woman—by turns elevated, fetishized, vilified—is a figure who bestrides the conventionally enforced boundaries of cultural forms. She exists to be shown, exchanged, and reproduced. Despite this insistence on the equivalency of the woman-as-represented as critical object, it is the forties advertising image which most interests me here, both as a cross-referential source for cinema studies and as an index to the shifting social tensions and economic priorities which fueled and helped shape all cultural utterances.[8]

The character of advertising/entertainment relations underwent significant and unprecedented alterations during the 1940s, particularly during the years 1941–1945. This half-decade constituted a unique moment in the history of representational forms in America, an epoch in which a contagion of advocacy, of the sort shrewdly engineered for several decades by the advertising industry, touched every mode of communication or entertainment. The hegemonic rule of the promotional imperative evidenced in these war years has never been duplicated in the annals of American cultural life.

A level of rhetorical urgency is distinguishable within an array of cultural expressions of the period, an urgency rooted in the experience of a nation and its shared values under siege. For World War II was, in Studs Turkel's phrase, the last "good war," the last time that anything like a consensus of thought and deed prevailed in a land of diversity. This unity of purpose is vividly illustrated in a Philco ad image from a *Life* magazine of October 1943 (fig. 1). Worker, soldier, and homefront warrior mobilize a unified assault on the Axis foes. Of course, the worker is a man, despite the fact that six million women workers had, by the end of the war, entered the industrial workforce,[9] and all three figures are white; the image might be seen as a residual cultural utterance in contrast to the attempts at ideological groundbreaking evident in, for example, many WPA murals of the 1930s. Yet the cartoon is instructive for its simultaneous elevation and quarantine of the female participant, displaying an ambivalence everywhere apparent beneath the ardor of the wartime appeal to the American woman while suggesting the cultural boundaries within which postwar resettlement finds it resonance and justification. For, clearly, an empowered woman is the stipulated addressee of the ad, her potency enforced by word (the caption's "With Everything—Including the Kitchen Sink!") and image. The strong diagonal thrust of the woman's outstretched arms, caught at their apogee, suggests a force greater than her cohorts', while serving to isolate her from the paired men. She is a combatant wielding a weapon which has literally been torn from the home. Like the aproned figure who holds it aloft, the kitchen sink has been pressed into extraordinary service for the duration; both woman and appliance can look forward to more familiar tasks at war's end. Such an image affirms a normative and residual vision even as it marks out its terrain of (temporary) difference.

It is important to mention that the focus here on the examination of forties promotional strategies and their bearing upon the woman as representational form in no way excludes the discussion of film and photography, given the extent to which the promotional gesture invaded all of representation. Social theorist Ernesto Laclau has developed the concept of ruptural unity to describe the combined characteristics of atypicality and popular consensus which govern social relations under Fascist rule.[10] This notion of ruptural unity applies in modified form to American life during the war years, a time of sacrifice and communality. Labor foreswore its chief tool, the strike; the corporate ranks offered their brightest executives for a dollar a year; and women took jobs in the fields—with the Women's

Land Army or U.S. Crop Corps—and in the factories. All for the Duration. Contemporary newsreel images, like those used in Connie Field's *The Life and Times of Rosie the Riveter* (1980), found their fictional echoes in such films of female service and self-sacrifice as *Tender Comrade* (1943) and *Since You Went Away* (1944).

Examples abound of the manner in which Hollywood films and photographic images functioned as persuasive cogs in the American war machine with a fervor equal to that of the straightforward war-promotional ad. Shot in 1941, released in early 1942, MGM's *Journey for Margaret* (1942) publicized the plight of the British people, particularly its homeless children. Margaret O'Brien's waifdom was intended as a spur to conscience. When, upon first sight of the bright lights of New York after months of London blackouts, little Margaret asks if America is fighting too, her adopted father Robert Young responds "Soon." Strains of "America the Beautiful" are heard over the fade-out. In like manner, a Prudential Life Insurance ad (fig. 2), published in *Life* magazine nine months prior to Pearl Harbor, evokes a kindred emotion, a call for compassion and reinforced national security. This is, of course, the insurance company's appropriation of the iconography of war relief; the father has been stricken uninsured. But it is certain that this appeal echoes the earliest anti-isolationist outcries for safety through preparedness. The open face and upturned eyes of the little girl denote an absolute vulnerability born of dispossession, even as the doll she clutches underscores her identity as embryonic mother and replicator of the species. The notions of homefront defense and species survival were thus joined indissolubly through the figure of the female, constituting a paternalist motivation capable of selling insurance or, a few months later, sending men off to war in a distant land.

Yet another advertising image (fig. 3) offers an unintended foreshadowing of that familiar wartime melodramatic trope, the tearful railroad station farewell. Appearing in March 1941, the ad promotes confidence in a benign technology (the Pullman car) that combines "home-like comforts" with peak efficiency. This scene of familial separation, cheerfully undertaken, would be replayed endlessly in a minor key in a host of Hollywood films of the mid-forties (recall the Jennifer Jones/Robert Walker good-bye in *Since You Went Away*, a scene that inspired its parodic offshoot in *Airplane* [1980] several decades later). But the conditions which occasion this cheerful farewell—the assurance of safety, the luxury of the accommodations, and the temporary character of the separation—will be reversed in dramatic fashion in a few short months. As in the case of the Prudential ad and so many others, the advertising image rehearses the salient imagery (particularly familial scenes) of the wartime experience to come, while promoting habits of consumption soon to be seriously circumscribed. Indeed, many of the wartime images—linked in popular memory to the special conditions of war—can be viewed as scenes "reinvested" by the heightened drama of wartime participation and personal sacrifice.

The assumption here, then, is of a measure of equivalency and mutual influence among image forms as fodder for wartime aims. Certainly, the Office of War Information and the War Manpower Commission took every opportunity to insure the participation of the imagemakers and the opinion-shapers.[11] Under the aegis of the War Advertising Council, an estimated half to three-quarters of all magazine ads dealt with war issues; a billion dollars' worth of advertising space and time was donated to War Advertising Council projects by war's end.[12] A succession of ad

Figure 1.

campaigns to encourage female participation in the labor force used direct mail or door-to-door solicitation at the community level, while advertising space was frequently donated for nationwide efforts, as, for example, enlistment into the Women's Army Auxiliary Corps (WAAC). Oftentimes, advertising space was devoted to morale-building or heartening messages with the corporate logo and often a mention of the company's own efforts attached. Greyhound buses sped the fighting men from post to post and would someday bring them home again.

More fanciful claims often suggested that consumption of a given product was a patriotic act, a phenomenon exemplified by a 1944 Kellogg's Corn Flakes ad which announced in boldface: "Assigned to 'Special Duty' in wartime meals!— Government nutritional authorities advise you to serve cereals more often for breakfast, lunch, supper. They save time, fuel, other foods." The two-page spread featured a series of separate panels most of which depicted women engaged in various labors. One smiling female figure, clad in the white uniform of a nurse, loomed above the rest, bestowing an aura of medical authority upon the company's claims. On the extreme left of the ad, a cheerful young woman held a bowl of Kellogg's chest high; the clock struck 7:00 over her shoulder while the caption beneath announced "Save time—they're ready to eat! Every minute counts in wartime. . ." Another panel offered the image of a woman welder hard at work, complete with goggles, a welding torch, and a trace of lipstick. The message beneath spoke of the "whole grain nutritive value" of the corn flakes and its compliance with the standards of the "new U.S. Official Nutrition Program." Other

Figure 2.   Figure 3.

illustrated claims included the work-saving value of Kellogg's products ("No pans, skillets to wash!") and their potential as a "meat-extender" when added to meat loaf, hamburger, or croquettes. The ad offers evidence of the proliferation of female roles enforced by the conditions of wartime life and the splitting of work commitments between home and workplace. While the purchase, preparation, and presentation of foodstuffs remained woman's work, the promotional appeals of the food industry now stressed time economy, ease of preparation, and thrift as a function of availability rather than purchasing power. For rationing inverted the customary relations between levels of consumption and social status. Such restraints on commodity acquisition—reinforced by government and industry alike—produced an ever-deepening reservoir of desire (rationalized as consumerist demand) that took years to assuage. Indeed, the dramatic expansion of the American economy and the cultural forms it spawned (see Mary Beth Haralovich's "Sitcoms and Suburbs" in this issue) are unthinkable without this four-year period of deferred gratification which industry helped to promulgate.

Peacetime rewards thus surpassed the return of the warrior; the onslaught of kitchen-centered commodity durables by 1946 was the woman's special prize. The transition was precipitous. The woman praised by the oil companies for her reluctance to consume in November 1943 (fig. 4) found herself elbow deep in a new deep-freeze unit by December 1945 (fig. 5)—a model that, to our eyes, looks more film cartridge than freezer. By 1946, the strictures of self-sacrifice were to be ended through the benevolence of Norge, Hotpoint, and Maytag; the pent-up desire to buy previously unavailable commodities with the capital accumulated through countless overtime hours was to be satisfied in full.

Figure 4.

Figure 5.

The woman was clearly targeted as the subject of this corporate address as she had been at least since the twenties. American industry clung to the fiction of female dependency (with women the grateful recipients of male benefaction) despite the statistics which showed that two-thirds of wartime women workers were employed prior to Pearl Harbor.[13] By May 1946, the female had become the vortex of a technological constellation, the orbit of applied science her newfound halo, promising a high-powered, streamlined future if only she would entrust her pocketbook to Bendix (fig. 6). In the same year, Westinghouse took the argument a step further, placing the commodity itself at stage center (fig. 7). But the pink scroll beneath the circular image and the display of female-identified goods surrounding it establish the appliance as a metonym for the woman whose touch has just now unlocked the bounties of refrigerated living.

In an effort to organize a massive volume of such material as well as to chart the broadest tendencies of woman-centered advertising images and their filmic and photographic counterparts, a general typology has been assembled. The categories of female-representational images have been grouped beneath two major headings on the basis of their principal character as object- or subject-oriented. The object orientation refers to an appropriation of the woman as a rhetorical or aesthetic figure for an audience which may or may not be targeted as female, while the subject orientation is a rubric which groups those representations addressed to a specifically female audience, either for purposes of enlistment to war service or incitement to consumption. The ads of the latter, subject-oriented grouping are significant less for the rhetorical strategies employed within them than for the dynamics of spectator engagement which they mobilize. Historically, these categories intermingle,

Figure 6.   Figure 7.

with no clearly defined temporal progression discernible. A final grouping represents a kind of supercession of the dyadic structure. It occurs precisely at the peak moment of backlash against the emergent woman and the standardization of "noir" typing—that is, the postwar cusp—1945–46. Here, subject/object distinctions collapse insofar as the woman is simultaneously and with equal forcefulness both addressed and objectified. In the representations of this meta-category, the American female was encouraged to identify with a self-image that was, literally, a distended and truncated one. This reordering of cultural signs was evidenced in every expressive form, quite dramatically in the Hollywood film. The advertising images of the period are, however, less mediated through narrative conventions and more graphic owing to their singularity of purpose—salesmanship. In terms suggested by Roland Barthes in his study of the photographic message, the advertising lexis is an elaborately encoded, fully "invested" cultural object.[14] It is an individuated unit of signification which invites its decipherment through a play of the familiar and the opaque. The best of these message packets impress themselves upon memory and, in retrospect, afford insight into the epistemological dissonances of a culture. The study of these images is thus a valuable supplement to the ideological analysis of postwar cinema.

The object orientation, the appropriation of the woman as figure, is, in large measure, transhistorical. A March 3, 1941, *Life* cover (fig. 8) is self-consciously derivative of a fundamental gesture of the patriarchal mythos—the gendered shaping of the sublime, the woman as pure form, wrought by the hand or tongue of man. As such, she assumes a metaphoric fullness, an aesthetic atopia. She can be used as a boost to value, her body contours expropriated to eroticize commodities or

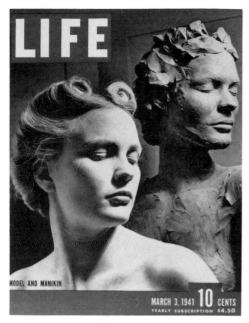

Figure 8.   Figure 9.

work processes. There, poised at the very threshold of the decade, *Life's* model/manikin strains to evoke an image of woman cleansed of all personal or historical markers. This is the essence of woman, the Masterpiece that Barthes has spoken of as the replica which jams the slide of the duplicative chain.[15] The image contains its own citation ("Beauty cannot assert itself save in the form of a citation")[16] but to an antiquity which yields to an anterior code. It is an image of silence ("There is only one way to stop the replication of beauty: hide it, return it to silence, to the ineffable, to aphasia")[17]—one that serves its master well. For if the ideal feminine is beauty unspeakable, it is equally beauty unable to speak; the muteness of the image insures its versatility as purveyor of wares and of values.

With the call to arms, fetishism went to war. Each star plucked from Gypsy Rose Lee's body by willing male patriots equaled a contribution to British War Relief, while a pair of Betty Grable's stockings fetched a war auction price of $40,000. The common theme of a series of 1942 war posters was the violation of the American woman (fig. 9). The process of male response evoked by these images of bondage and mutilation can only remain a source of speculation. One possible reading: a furious and destructive libidinal drive is projected onto the Other, German or Japanese, which demands to be doubly punished—first, as a denial of unrepresentable male desire unchecked by psyche or society and, secondly, as vengeance for the primordial robbery of the woman, nexus of exchange and aesthetic value within the culture.

The female form was drafted into patriotic service in less inflammatory fashion as well. Two *Life* photostories, in June and November 1943, suggested that bare backs and shoulders were an admirable gesture of self-sacrifice, freeing fabric for more

Figure 10.

Figure 11.

essential duty. A September 1943 Dixie Cup ad (fig. 10) fused product allocation with female devotion; a hybrid figure—part drinking vessel, part woman—coos her pledge of fidelity to a thirsty sailor. At about the same time, Preston Sturges was engaged in his own examination of sexualized service in *The Miracle of Morgan's Creek* (1943). Betty Hutton's commitment to kiss the boys goodbye, all the boys, is, like the Dixie Cup pledge, a dedication to the war effort which postulated promiscuity as patriotism. The sly satire of the Sturges film succeeds here, as in *Hail the Conquering Hero* (1945), in the defamiliarizing of wartime virtues and the obsessive valorization of motherhood.

For, indeed, the appropriation of the female was not limited to its eroticizing function; the maternal was another frequently invoked valence of the woman. *Life* photographer Robert Capa's famous mourning mothers of Naples (appearing in the November 8, 1943, issue) eternalized the lament for all lost sons, condensing and purging a depth of grief experienced by both men and woman in wartime, an image the more deeply etched for its relay of emotion through the suffering woman with its myriad art-historical references. In that same issue of *Life*, Alfred Eisenstadt's portrait of the lonely widow and mother from his photoessay, "An American Block," furnished an emblem of spiritual fortitude not far removed from the indomitability of the maternal embodied in Greer Garson's Kay Miniver. William Wyler's 1942 release, *Mrs. Miniver*, eulogizes Britain at war and the moral toughness of its

Figure 12.   Figure 13.

people, a strength rooted in matriarchy. It is the function of Kay Miniver to reinvigorate the fading aristocracy represented by the Beldon women through an injection of a moral nobility attained in homefront combat. The virtues of patience and maternal nurturance could be coupled with the power to act; *Mrs. Miniver's* florid optimism earned it the universal praise of the day. But motherhood had other uses. There was, after all, much to be gained from the invocation of a mother's anxiety (fig. 11); guilt was a powerful weapon in the wartime arsenal.

Women were, throughout the war years, the subjects of a cultural address issuing from a variety of sources serving a multitude of purposes. Government directives and fashion trends, indeed, cultural images of every sort evidenced a potential for reversibility and instant contradiction during this volatile period. If, in 1941, Veronica Lake's peek-a-boo hairstyle was the stuff of glamour, two years later, in Bud Fraker's photograph which Paramount dutifully supplied to news services, the same hairstyle was portrayed as an industrial saboteur threatening productivity. (In the photograph, Lake's luxurious tresses are entangled in a drill press; ornamental adornment must give way to the upswept or turbaned look better suited to the industrial workplace.) Signs of direct address to the women were everywhere apparent; an imperative mood prevailed. The alphabet soup of government agencies supplied a steady stream of behavioral and moral injunctions for the home front. A telling sign of the unified and intensified rhetoric of public address during wartime was the flow of informational, entertainment, and promotional messages routinely delivered in a centralized and authoritative second person. A three-page photo essay appearing in *Life*'s Christmas 1942 issue offers illustration of this imperative mood. Entitled "Don't Travel!," the piece warned all potential travel-

Figure 14.   Figure 15.

ers—except soldiers and businessmen—to stay home for the holidays. The implicit message to women, many of whom wished to reunite families for the holidays, was that their emotional needs were to be sacrificed to the "essential" business of war. A virtual unanimity of purpose and the universal participation of news organs, advertisers, and film studios produced a levelling of cultural forms with regard to both tone and content. A measure of stridency and the interjection of self-contained war appeals marked Hollywood's releases prior to June of 1942 and the turning point in the Pacific at the Battle of Midway, e.g. *Joe Smith, American* (1942); *Pacific Blackout* (1941); *Star-Spangled Rhythm* (1942); *Priorities on Parade*, (1942).

In *Priorities on Parade*, Paramount ingenue Betty Rhodes plays a welder in an aircraft factory who has occasion to deliver a one-sentence message directly to the camera: "But it's getting to be the smart thing to do for girls to get in there and pitch too, whatever way they can." As I have argued elsewhere,[18] this structuring of address constitutes an instance of interpellation, a notion developed by Louis Althusser in his seminal essay, "Ideology and Ideological State Apparatuses," to denote the "hailing" or beckoning power which ideology exercises over concrete human subjects.[19] Traces of a proliferation and intensification of direct address, that is, of an interpellative urgency, are entirely consistent with the increased reciprocity of ideas—those culturally transmitted and those government-circulated—characteristic of the early war years.

A principal component of the war culture of the forties, then, was the blurring of distinctions between normally enforced domains—between public and private sectors, between advertising copy and journalistic reportage, and between war promotion and self-promotion in product ads. In all phases of image production

Figure 16.

Figure 17.

and transmission, however, the address to the female subject remained a dominant, highly visible strategy. A Fleishmann's yeast ad of December 1942 announced an end to frailty (fig. 12). Here, a gender-specific product addresses its female audience with a boldness and seriousness typical of the first dark days of the war. If the Fleischmann ad emphasized the new seriousness of woman's work, a number of contemporary image sources reminded women of the necessity for vigilance on the cosmetic front as well. An Alfred Eisenstadt photoessay, "An American Block" (*Life*, November 8, 1943), included a photographic portrait of Janet Fritz, local glamour girl, preparing for an evening of volunteer duty as a nurse's aide. In time of war, a uniform offered no curb to fashion. A strong current of mid-war promotion reinforced the idea that a woman's toughness and resilience was not unglamourous. A series of Du Barry cosmetic ads (fig. 13) applauded the efforts of servicewomen who remained radiant despite the rigors of their work and the sacrifice of traditional feminine attire. A fresh-faced blonde sporting a paramilitary look (fig. 14) shovels a spoonful of Shredded Ralston into her smiling face from the back cover of a *Liberty* magazine of April 1944. Eating cereal from a red, white, and blue box is always a patriotic act during a war; the promotion of female enlistment only adds luster to the Ralston Company's good citizenship. A second *Liberty* back cover of the same month (fig. 15) was adorned with yet another standard figure from the wartime inventory of "good girl" images. This woman, like all faithful lovers and wives, is a tireless correspondent and confidant who also cares enough to share a good smoke. Implicit to these images of commodity consumption is a modelling of female behavior intended to benefit the national effort.

Often the manufacturer/advertiser's tone was patronizing, scolding those who

Figure 18.   Figure 19.

shirked their share of duty like the recalcitrant pigtailer. Note the vehemence of Scott Tissue's argument for its status as an essential industry supplying a vital link in the chain of public health ("Toilet Tissue is the Simple Essential upon which American Plumbing and Therefore Public Health Depends," fig. 16). It is from this stable perch that Scott deigned to lecture, not the genderless teenager, but the young woman in need of domestic training. A familiar litany of wartime slogans (Womanpower, production line, the blitz, war-work) were mobilized in the interest of soliciting the cheerful participation of young women as a substitute domestic labor force (the *girl* behind the woman behind the man behind the gun). Admirable were the hard-working and true-spirited females, blissfully apotheosized in the "*Mademoiselle* Merit Awards" given by that magazine to "the ten young women who designed 1944 for living." The last citation of the ten was a posthumous award to Lady, Marine War Dog, who, as the only female member of the First War Dog Tactical Unit, gave her life that many American boys might live. Possessed of the ideal name for the task, Lady was the ultimate proof that females need not compromise the benefits of gender for rugged service. Even the meanest, toughest Leatherneck canine of them all could be a Lady fit for the pages of *Mademoiselle*.

The predominant strain of address to the postwar woman was toward unmitigated consumption but within a restrictive, domesticated sphere. The first wave of ad images heralded the matrimonial state as the consummation and reward for all prior efforts. The most colorful of these campaigns was mounted by Oneida's Community line of silverplated cutlery, featuring a series of full-page ads of a

Figure 20.   *Figure 21.*

Loretta Young look-alike enjoying the highlights of her special day when, in the words of the ad, "one plus one equals one" (fig. 17). Like Oneida's silverplate, this state of matrimonial bliss is said to be "for keeps." Once again, wish replaces lived experience; in the first four years of the turbulent forties, the divorce rate had nearly doubled.[20]

Concurrent with the wedding focus was, of course, the paean to the baby. The January 21, 1946, issue of *Life* heralded the newest *March of Time* newsreel release, entitled "Life With Baby." This was, indeed, a "movie for the millions." More disquieting by far was the sense one has of an effort to convince the American woman that motherhood would, of necessity, be a full-time job which would brook no competition from a second career. Only with the help of American industry and medical science could a mother hope to master her new calling. Of course, while marriage and motherhood exalted the postwar woman to a regal state, domestic labor was acknowledged as her constant companion. A harrowing image from a 1947 issue of *Life* offered illustration of one full year's worth of woman's work. A humbly clad figure stands in the midground of a bleak panorama, broom in hand. Before her are arrayed countless stacks of dishes to be washed, neat rows of

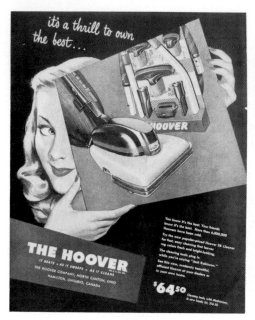

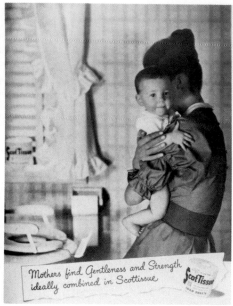

Figure 22.   Figure 23.

silverware to be polished, and barrels of raw food to be cooked. Behind her a sea of beds-to-be-made stretch toward the deep-focus vanishing point while above her a Damoclean sword of domesticity (a laden clothesline) hangs menacingly. The woman's lone mechanical ally is a sturdy-looking washing machine. Little wonder that an endless stream of ad images offered the services of labor-saving devices to lighten the load—and keep the peacetime economy operating at full capacity. The good fortune of a woman could be measured by the tonnage of her sparkling new appliances and by the luxury items which were her special reward.

I have reserved until the end the most disturbing and, no doubt, most complex category of postwar female imagery referred to earlier as constituting a supercession of the dyadic subject/object structuring principle. The images of this grouping offer evidence of that loss of social ground and self-definition which helped form "noir" characterizations on the one hand and the overly demure, lobotomized female representations of postwar culture.[21] The represented female of this image category is characteristically veiled, distorted, or disproportionate to the surrounding field of objects. These deforming images, far from imposing pure objecthood or an exclusion of female subjectivity, are, without exception, targeted for and addressed to a female consumer.

The compositional and iconographic elements of an ad for Freshy playclothes appearing in the January 1945 issue of *Mademoiselle* (fig. 18), despite its light-flooded veneer, resonate with the filmic inscriptions of the seductive and homicidal female—the spiderweb configurations of *Out of the Past* (1947) or the windowless soul effect familiar from *Double Indemnity* (1944) or *Leave Her to Heaven* (1945) in which dark glasses signify inscrutability of motive and, ultimately, a moral abyss.

Figure 24.

Figure 25.

Figure 26.   Figure 27.

The veil as sign of modesty, discernible in mid-war ads, gives way to a shadowy, broader-brimmed look (fig. 19) that beings to darken considerably by 1946 (fig. 20). The imposition of shadow or pattern upon the woman's face obscures or scars its surface, shifting and unsettling moral valences, an effect echoed in such *films noirs* as *Double Indemnity, The Killers* (1946), *The Dark Mirror* (1946), and *The Locket* (1946).

Another observable trend in ad images was the truncation of the female body or the partial replacement of the head by objects whose referential ties were culturally binding (figs. 21–23): the woman as precious object suitable for collection; the Hoover-head; or mother-woman. These hybrid bodies call to mind Ellen Berent of *Leave Her to Heaven* (fig. 24), who is unvisaged in our first sighting of her, her own head replaced by the image of the man she will pathologically desire and attempt to destroy.[22] The metaphorical violence done the represented female body in so many postwar images is notably directed against the woman's head rather than the conventionally eroticized zones of leg or breast. For the attack upon the American female during this period engendered, in the most fundamental terms, a radical disorientation of identity and collective consciousness. Besieged on every side by

Figure 28.

the bold address of cultural directives seeking voluntary abdication from the seat of her new-found power, the American postwar woman can best be imaged as the subject of a radical split or dissociation, exemplified by the January 1945 cover of *Mademoiselle* (fig. 25).

But the most insidious misogyny of all is to be found in a Johnson & Johnson ad campaign for its baby-care products which appeared in the pages of *Life* for more than two years, from 1946 well into 1948 (figs. 26, 27). The common thread among these images is the thorough-going humiliation of the mother at the hands of the male child. In each instance, a Brobdingnagian boy-child, empowered by a primitive matting process, wreaks his vengeance upon the helpless woman whose only sin has been an unwillingness to purchase the skincare products of Johnson & Johnson. Various forms of torture are enacted which depend upon the inversion of size relations so that the shrunken mother is forced to endure the privations of infantile dependency while the baby man rehearses male authority. The ad copy inevitably narrates a process of capitulation and recantation so that the offense to child and corporation is simultaneously redressed. It is no wonder that the much-maligned mother-consumer was, by July 1948 (fig. 28), reduced in spirit and scope of creative outlet to the refrigeration of Milky Way bars. The mirthless grin of the model testifies to the betrayal of female potential, the foreclosure of a culture's promises to half its people.

That betrayal was, in fact, a historical process, a construction within ideology which summoned forth the complicity of all, in varying degrees. The analysis of the underlying social and economic forces which shaped the postwar era and the precise relationship of these forces to cultural phenomena remain subjects of signal importance for the study of film as popular culture. My own purpose here has been to lay the conceptual and practical groundwork for an expanded notion of the intertextual domain within which female representation came to occupy a position of privilege within the American cinema of the 1940s. By suggesting the necessity for the further examination of coextensive systems of representation, I have sought to push the limits of a too-frequently parochial understanding of cultural determination within the realm of film studies. While I have argued for a greater concern for the Mode of Cultural Production in a broad sense, I have limited myself to the survey of a particular species of forties cultural currency: the woman as representable within a trio of overlapping idioms—advertising, photojournalism, and cinema. That others share this interest in the development of what Raymond Williams has termed cultural materialism with its attendant concern both for the specificities of particular cultural practices and for their placement within a larger arena of social forces is made evident by the ground-breaking work contained elsewhere in this special issue. The promise of such a "cultural studies" approach is the enrichment of our sense of the broad range of cultural/material determinations within which any film—any cultural or aesthetic object—comes to be formed (by its producers) and comprehended (by its recipients).

NOTES

1. Stuart Ewen, *Captains of Consciousness: Advertising and the Social Roots of the Consumer Culture* (New York: McGraw-Hill, 1976), p. 19.
2. Raymond Williams, *Marxism and Literature* (Oxford: Oxford University Press, 1977), pp. 83–89.
3. Terry Eagleton, *Criticism & Ideology* (London: Verso Editions, 1978), p. 44.
4. Roland Barthes, *S/Z*, trans. Richard Miller (New York: Hill and Wang, 1974), p. 5.
5. Ibid., p. 20.
6. Ibid., p. 21.
7. Karl Marx, *Capital*, trans. Samuel Moore and Edward Aveling (New York: International Publishers, 1967), p. 66.
8. By way of contemporary update, there should be no doubt of the scale and ubiquity of the advertising presence in our midst or the durability of advertising's relationship to cinematic practice. One need only consider the encroachment of advertising within the ranks of public broadcasting or the monumental successes of MTV's nonstop promotion of artists and records or of a rock musical such as *Purple Rain* (1984). The tie-ins and overlapping formats of that blockbuster as film, album, and rock video constituted each format as a promotional lure for its other constituent parts. Further proof of this notion of the accelerating convergence of advertising and entertainment image-making is offered by the remarks of Coca-Cola Chairman Roberto C. Goizueta, who expressed amazement at the importance attached to the hiring and firing of studio executives at Coca-Cola subsidiary Columbia Pictures in the wake of its acquisition. "I feel there is too much made . . . about what it takes to handle a creative endeavor. You have to admit that a good Coca-Cola commercial is pretty

much of a creative endeavor, and yet it's been handled by management of the company year in and year out." Goizueta went on to announce plans to begin test distributions of Columbia releases on videocassettes through Coca-Cola bottlers and in Japanese supermarkets by January 1985. In the eyes of the latter-day corporate moguls, the image—advertising or entertainment—is a commodity to be marketed and distributed with utmost efficiency.

9. Eleanor Straub, "Government Policy Toward Civilian Women During World War II," Ph.D. dissertation, Emory University, 1973, p. 36.

10. Ernesto Laclau, *Politics & Ideology in Marxist Theory* (London: Verso Editions, 1977), pp. 92–93.

11. The Roosevelt administration saw to it that corporate patriotism was also sound business practice. With an excess profits tax delivering eighty-five cents on many a corporate dollar to government coffers, advertising—ruled tax deductible by a stroke of Roosevelt-style pragmatism—was viewed as a long-term marketing tool available at bargain rates.

12. Raymond Rubicam, "Advertising," in *While You Were Gone*, ed. Jack Goodman (New York: Simon and Schuster, 1946), p. 427.

13. Straub, op. cit., pp. 142–143.

14. Roland Barthes, "The Photographic Message," in *Image/Music/Text* trans. Stephen Heath (New York: Hill and Wang, 1977), p. 20.

15. Barthes, *S/Z*, p. 115.

16. Ibid., p. 33.

17. Ibid., p. 34.

18. Michael Renov, "The State, Ideology, and *Priorities on Parade*," *Film Reader* 5 (1982): 216–226.

19. Louis Althusser, "Ideology and Ideological State Apparatuses," in *Lenin and Philosophy*, trans. Ben Brewster (New York: Monthly Review Press, 1971), p. 174.

20. J.E. Trey, "Women in the War Economy—World War II," *The Review of Radical Political Economics* 4, no. 3 (Summer 1972): 48.

21. For a gloss on the relevance of the lobotomy in this context, see Mary Jane Ward's novel *The Snake Pit* or Anatole Litvak's 1948 film version along with any literary or filmic account of the life of Frances Farmer.

22. For a more complete treatment of the implications of this introductory image of the Gene Tierney character, see my "*Leave Her to Heaven*: The Double Bind of the Post-War Woman," *Journal of the University Film and Video Association* 35, no. 1 (Winter 1983): 28–36. She is seated on board a train, across from the man whose book she reads, the man who will become her idée fixe. Her own head—locus of the psyche—is here already replaced by the represented image of the man-in-print, the one who possesses and governs the power of symbolic utterance.

Quar. Rev. of Film & Video, Vol. 11, pp. 23–33
Reprints available directly from the publisher
Photocopying permitted by license only

Harwood Academic Publishers, 1989
Printed in the United States of America

The Economy of Desire: The Commodity Form in/of the Cinema

Mary Ann Doane

Much of feminist theory tends to envisage the woman's relation to the commodity in terms of "being" rather than "having": she is the object of exchange rather than its subject.[1] What is invoked here is the asubjectivity of the commodity. The woman's objectification, her susceptibility to processes of fetishization, display, profit and loss, the production of surplus value, all situate her in a relation of resemblance to the commodity form. As Fredric Jameson points out, ". . . by its transformation into a commodity a thing, of whatever type, has been reduced to a means for its own consumption. It no longer has any qualitative value in itself, but only insofar as it can be 'used'. . . ."[2] But the status of the woman as commodity in feminist theory is not merely the result of a striking metaphor or parallel. Its elaboration is a response to Lévi-Strauss's description of the exchange of women as nothing less than the foundation of human society, of culture—the guarantee of an exogamy without which the family, and society along with it, would suffer an incestuous collapse.

The notion of the woman as the Ur-object of exchange has been taken up by theorists such as Luce Irigaray and subjected to a parodic over-writing in essays such as "When the Goods Get Together" and "Women on the Market."[3] From this perspective, Marx's analysis of value and of the commodity as the elementary form of capitalist wealth is understood as an accurate although displaced interpretation of the status of women in a patriarchal society.

In our social order, women are 'products' used and exchanged by men. Their status is that of merchandise, 'commodities'. . . . So women have to remain an 'infrastructure' unrecognized as such by society and our culture. The use, consumption, and circulation of their sexualized bodies underwrite the organization and reproduction of the social order, in which they have never taken part as 'subjects.'[4]

The erasure of female subjectivity by the commodification of the female body is, however, never quite successful. Just as Lévi-Strauss, despite his attempt to compare the exchange of women to the exchange of words, must admit that women also speak, the feminist theorist must acknowledge the fact that women also buy. Not only do they buy but since the early years of the 20th century the woman has been situated by a capitalist economy as the prototype of the modern consumer. In the theorization of the commodification of the woman there is, therefore, a hitch—a

MARY ANN DOANE, *Associate Professor of Film and Semiotic Theory at Brown University, Providence, Rhode Island 02912. She is the author of articles on feminism, psychoanalysis, and film theory in leading film journals, as well as of the forthcoming book* The Desire to Desire: The Woman's Film of the 1940s.

hitch not unlike the one encountered by Lévi-Strauss. Much to his dismay, the anthropologist discovers that the woman "must be recognized as a generator of signs."[5] But Lévi-Strauss makes an amazing comeback and recoups his losses by attaching the woman's "talent, before and after marriage, for taking her part in a duet"[6] to an intensification of the affective value of sexual relations—to that "affective richness, ardour and mystery" which originally characterized all signs-to-be-exchanged, not just the woman. This leaves the woman with a fairly heavy burden of affect. I would like to argue here that the woman's ability to purchase, her subjectivity as a consumer, is qualified by a relation to commodities which is also ultimately subordinated to that intensification of the affective value of sexual relations which underpins a patriarchal society. In other words, Irigaray's theory of the woman as commodity and the historical analysis of the woman's positioning as consumer—as subject rather than object of the commodity form—are only apparently contradictory. But this involves both rethinking the absoluteness of the dichotomy between subject and object which informs much feminist thinking and analyzing the ways in which the woman is encouraged to actively participate in her own oppression.

Of course it is only insofar as consumerism is associated with a particularly maligned form of subjectivity or agency that the woman's role in such an exchange is assured. As Jameson points out, ". . . the conception of the mindless consumer, the ultimate commodified 'false consciousness' of shopping-centre capitalism, is a conception of 'otherness'. . . . degraded consumption is assigned to women, to what used to be called 'Mrs. American Housewife.' "[7] The degradation here is linked to the idea of the consumer as a passive subject who is taken in by the lure of advertising, the seduction of the image. In other words, the phenomenon of consumerism is conceptualized in terms which are not far from those used to delineate spectatorship in the cinema. The film frame functions, in this context, not as a "window on the world" as in the Bazinian formulation, but as a quite specific kind of window—a shop window. Or, as Charles Eckert points out with reference to the short films of the first decade of the century, ". . . they functioned as living display windows for all that they contained; windows that were occupied by marvelous mannequins and swathed in a fetish-inducing ambiance of music and emotion."[8] The relation between the cinema and consumerism is buttressed by the film's capability for representing not merely objects but objects in their fetishized form as commodities. The glamour, the sheen of the cinema and its stars metonymically infect the objects of the mise-en-scène. As Jeanne Allen claims, the spectator is encouraged to desire the possession of a material environment, an environment which "represented a standard of living promised to the viewer ideologically, but awarded only to the eye."[9] Or, as Will Hays put it in a 1930 radio speech, "The motion picture carries to every American at home, and to millions of potential purchasers abroad, the visual, vivid perception of American manufactured products."[10] It would be quite appropriate, it seems, to apply Laura Mulvey's phrase, "to-be-looked-at-ness," to the filmic object in its transformation into a commodity as well as to the woman as spectacle.

One can isolate at least three instances of the commodity form in its relation to the cinema and the question of the female spectator-consumer. The first is fully consistent with Irigaray's analysis of the woman as commodity in a patriarchal system of exchange and involves the encouragement of the woman's narcissistic apprehension of the image of the woman on the screen. The female spectator is invited to witness her own commodification and, furthermore, to buy an image of herself insofar as the female star is proposed as the ideal of feminine beauty. "Buying" here is belief—the image has a certain amount of currency. This level involves not only the currency of a body but of a space in which to display that body: a car, a house, a room filled with furniture and appliances. The second type of relation between the commodity form and the cinema is in some ways the most direct—the commodity tie-in which often involves a contractual agreement between the manufacturer and the studio. The result may be the subtle or not so subtle placement of a Coca-Cola logo or other brand name in the background of a scene. As the most explicit link between the commodity form and the cinema, this type of display has historically been subjected to a great deal of criticism. Such criticism is then deflected to some extent away from the movie industry when the commodity is "tied in" in a space off-screen by linking a line of clothing, for instance, to a particular film or associating a star with a specific product. This process serves to mediate the spectator's access to the ideal image on the screen. It disperses the fascination of the cinema onto a multiplicity of products whose function is to allow the spectator to approximate that image. Finally, the third instance of commodity form in the cinematic institution concerns the film itself and its status as a commodity in a circuit of exchange. The film in its commodity form promotes a certain mode of perception which is fully adequate to a consumer society and which, for the female spectator, initiates a particularly complex dialectic of "being," "having," and "appearing." Michèle Le Doeuff has, quite legitimately, warned us about the metaphorical use of the term "economy" in contemporary theory—the resort to phrases such as "libidinal economy," "textual economy," "classical economy," "general economy"—a usage which absolves the theorist from a confrontation with the economy "proper" insofar as it refers to such things as prices, exchanges, markets.[11] However, the injunction negates the profound connections between the different economies, a connection which is, perhaps, most visible in the cinema. The economy of the text, its regulation of spectatorial investments and drives, is linked to the economy of tie-ins, the logic of the female subject's relation to the commodity—her status as consumer of goods and consumer of discourses.

The development of the cinematic institution is frequently associated with the rise of consumerism. Overproduction toward the end of the 19th century together with Henry Ford's development of "line production" in 1910 and the intensification of production during World War I led to a situation in which there was an excess of material goods and a scarcity of consumers, a condition necessitating the perfection of advertising and marketing strategies geared toward a mass audience. Positioning the laborer as a consumer was also an effective means of countering an emerging resistance to the industrial and corporate structure on the part of workers.[12] As Judith Mayne points out in her study of immigrant audiences, ". . . consumerism offered the image of an homogeneous population pursuing the same goals—'living well' and accumulating goods. The movie theater seemed to offer an ideal space for the exhibition of this image, for workers and eventually middle-class people needed only to pay a small admission price in order to share equally in the spectacle offered on the screen."[13] And it would seem that the spectator-consumer was increasingly envisaged as female. Jeanne Allen notes how, as early as 1916, Paramount's promotional journal printed an article describing "the way in which fashionable women derive ideas for interior decoration by copying the sets presented in films."[14] Furthermore, as Allen points out, the space of the theater itself was conceived as specifically feminine: "A 1927 article in *Theatre Management*, for example, stressed the importance of women as the primary component and motivators of film attendance and argued that the appeal of both the film and the theater must be geared to pleasing women's sensibilities. Art works in the lobbies, attractive fabrics and designs for interior decoration, and subdued and flattering lighting were important appeals to women's tastes and to their desire for comfort and relaxation."[15] Fan magazines in their earliest incarnations are linked with the purportedly female obsession with stars, glamour, gossip, and fashionability. The much sought-after address to the female spectator often seems more readily accessible in the discursive apparatus surrounding the film than in the text itself.

In an article entitled "The Carole Lombard in Macy's Window," Charles Eckert sketches the history of the cinema's links to commodity fetishism, but he is most concerned with what he refers to as "the almost incestuous hegemony that characterized Hollywood's relations with vast reaches of the American economy by the mid-1930s."[16] What is striking about Eckert's account is the amount of space he must devote to the two genres of commodities which are most strongly evocative of female narcissism: fashion and cosmetics. Indeed, Eckert suggests that the projected audience for this "showcasing" of commodities was not at all heterogeneous in relation to such factors as age, sex, ethnicity, or marital status: "Out there, working as a clerk in a store and living in an apartment with a friend, was *one girl*— single, nineteen years old, Anglo-Saxon, somewhat favoring Janet Gaynor."[17] Eckert carefully traces the vicissitudes of fashion's intimate connection with Hollywood, from clothing lines such as "Miss Hollywood Junior" which exploited labels with a star's name and picture, to the brainchild of Bernard Waldman, the chain of Cinema Fashions shops, only one to a city, which sold copies of the gowns worn by stars in specific pictures. Although there were, in addition to such showcasing techniques, a very large number of commodity tie-ups which were not so gender specific—from watches to toothpaste, to desks, typewriters, and cars—the glamour, sheen, and fascination attached to the movie screen seemed most appropriate for the marketing of a certain feminine self-image.

The commodity tie-up or tie-in is usually closely associated with the materials prepared by the studio's publicity department in order to market the movie, materials which are gathered together in a publication referred to as the campaign book or press book and sent to exhibitors. In an article in *The Saturday Evening Post* in 1927, Carl Laemmle speaks of the press book primarily in terms of the marketing of the film itself as a commodity:

Three departments of advertising, publicity, and exploitation combined first on the preparation of the press book or campaign book. This constitutes a complete and encyclopedic guide to the local theater owner in selling the picture to his public. In effect, it places in the employ of the smallest theater owner in the country the services of the best possible advertising, publicity, and exploitation brains that we can secure.[18]

The press book even goes so far as to provide the "intimate, chatty type of copy so eagerly relished by the screen fans."[19] By the mid-1930s the press book has been perfected for the promotion not only of the movie itself but of a host of products connected in often extremely tangential ways to the film. In sections entitled, "Exploitation," the studio experts isolate a particular scene, condensed onto a publicity still (an arrival scene for example), and suggest its affiliation with the appropriate commodity (in this instance, luggage). Metonymy is the trope of the tie-in. The press book constitutes a detailed reading of the filmic text to produce the conditions of its own marketability as well as the conditions of a general consumerism which it invites and encourages. It works to disseminate the fetishism of the filmic image in a metonymic chain of commodities.

If the film frame is a kind of display window and spectatorship consequently a form of window-shopping, the intimate association of looking and buying does indeed suggest that the prototype of the spectator-consumer is female. And ultimately Eckert's argument is that the alliance between the cinema and the commodity form in a consumer-conscious society generates a genre of films explicitly addressed to the female spectator. As he points out, "Consumer statistics widely disseminated in the late 1920's and early 1930's show that women made 80 to 90 percent of all purchases for family use. They bought 48 percent of drugs, 96 percent of dry goods, 87 percent of raw products, 98 percent of automobiles."[20] The confluence of three different factors—the expanding awareness of the significant economic role of the female consumer, the industry's commitment to the development of commodity tie-ins, and a star system dominated by women—opened up a space for "a steady output of films dominated by starlets—those hundreds of 'women's films' which are of such interest to feminist critics like Haskell and Rosen."[21] The conditions of possibility of the woman's film as a genre are closely linked to the commodity form.

By the 1940s the system of tie-ins and press books was fully in place and the machinery of advertising had attained a fairly sophisticated form. Furthermore, the war served to reinforce the view that the spectator to be addressed is female. The film industry tended to operate under the assumption that the audience was composed primarily of women. In addition, audience analysis confirms that women were "usually better versed than men on movie topics."[22] Women were fully immersed in the discursive apparatus surrounding the cinema—fan magazines as well as news columns and articles on or by stars in women's magazines.

Advertising outside the context of the cinema, by this time a highly efficient machine designed to facilitate the circulation of commodities, was frequently subordinated to the ideological imperative of moving women first into and then out of the work force in a fairly short period of time (the "Rosie the Riveter" phenomenon). The commodity was at least a small part of the lure tempting the woman to take a job in the first place—the era of high consumerism had arrived and the new assessment of "economic need" persuaded the woman to work in order to maintain her standard of living. But the commodity was also activated as the lure back into the domestic space of the home in the postwar years when the threat of male unemployment was great. Even during the war, as Susan M. Hartmann notes, "General Electric predicted that women would welcome their return 'to the old housekeeping routine' because it would be transformed by new appliances. The Eureka Vacuum Cleaner Company praised its women on the assembly line, but promised that at war's end, 'like you, Mrs. America, Eureka will put aside its uniform and return to the ways of peace . . . building household appliances.'"[23] Advertising during the war provoked the reader to fantasize about the various types of commodities which would be available after the war—cars, houses, as well as furniture and household appliances.

What is amazing about advertising in this particular historical conjuncture is that it continues to operate at full force despite the absence of commodities—the scarcity of material goods imposed by a wartime economy. Undoubtedly this advertising without an object functions to insure that consumers do not forget brand names, causing advertisers to somehow lose their hold over their audience. But it also demonstrates how advertising, beyond the aim of selling a particular commodity, functions to generate and maintain an aptitude for consumption in the subject. A picture of a woman holding a Revere Copper-Clad Stainless Steel pan in front of a scene depicting an intense military battle is captioned with the apologetic statement, "Mrs. Parker's cooking utensils are making it hot for the Japs." A young woman clad only in a bra and a Lastex Real-Form panty girdle licks a food stamp and looks out provocatively at the reader beneath the phrase "Military Needs Come First."

This objectlessness of the advertising discourse frequently prompts a return to the female body as the prototypical object of commodity fetishism. "Rosie the Riveter" was conceived from the beginning as a temporary phenomenon, active only for the duration, and throughout the war years the female spectator-consumer was sold a certain image of femininity which functioned to sustain the belief that women and work outside the home were basically incompatible. The woman's new role in production was masked by an insistent emphasis upon a narcissistic consumption. She was encouraged to view herself as engaged in a constant battle to protect her femininity from the ravages of the workplace with the aid of a host of products: hand lotions, facial creams, mattresses, tampons. Furthermore, it was this idea of femininity that American soldiers were fighting to protect. This notion is most explicit in an ad for Tangee lipstick entitled "War, Women and Lipstick." Alongside of a photograph of a glamorous young female pilot emerging from a cockpit is the following text:

For the first time in history woman-power is a factor in war. Millions of you are fighting and working side by side with your men.

In fact, you are doing double duty—for you are still carrying on your traditional "woman's" work of cooking, and cleaning, and home-making. Yet, somehow, American women are still the loveliest and most spirited in the world. The best dressed, the best informed, the best looking.

It's a reflection of the free democratic way of life that you have succeeded in keeping your femininity—even though you are doing man's work!

If a symbol were needed of this fine, independent spirit—of this courage and strength—I would choose a lipstick. It is one of those mysterious little essentials that have an importance far beyond their size and cost.

A woman's lipstick is an instrument of personal morale that helps her to conceal heartbreak or sorrow; gives her self-confidence when it's badly needed; heightens her loveliness when she wants to look her loveliest.

No lipstick—ours or anyone else's—will win the war. But it symbolizes one of the reasons why we are fighting . . . the precious right of women to be feminine and lovely—under any circumstances.

Femininity was intimately articulated with a patriotic nationalism. It could also be argued that the Rosie the Riveter image (the original—parodic—Normal Rockwell painting on the cover of *The Saturday Evening Post*, where a Rosie with bulging muscles and a huge riveting gun across her lap crushes a copy of *Mein Kampf* beneath her heel) was chosen precisely for its effectiveness in demarcating the absoluteness of the antithesis between femininity and what continued to be considered as "men's work." Traditional ideas concerning femininity were crucial to the plethora of antifeminist discourses emerging after the war, reaching their apex in Lundberg and Farnham's *Modern Woman: The Lost Sex.*[24]

This aura of a femininity fully contained by a fetishized body image and its corresponding narcissism was also promoted in the press books designed to market and exploit the films of the 40s.[25] The woman's split subjectivity as worker and wife, or masculinized worker and the embodiment of femininity, is accompanied in the press book by a doubling of female types, subsumed beneath the overpowering category of beauty. A suggested promotional scheme associated with *A Stolen Life*, a film in which Bette Davis plays twin sisters, involves setting the claim "Every Woman Plays a Double Role" next to any one of the following advertisements: "Secretary and Siren—so delightfully *both* with a make-up kit from Maxine's"; "You're bright . . . You're blase . . . You're Both with Fashions from Georgia's Dress Shoppe," etc. The press book for *Dark Victory* (1939) is insistent about its potential audience: "*Dark Victory* is definitely a woman's picture and should be exploited as such via the woman's page of your local paper and in cooperation with women's shops." The suggestions include a translation of the film's two female stars, Bette Davis and Geraldine Fitzgerald, into two feminine types with two entirely different make-up needs: medium skin with blonde hair (Bette Davis) and fair skin with dark hair (Geraldine Fitzgerald). The press book for *The Two Mrs. Carrolls* (1947) employs a similar strategy by encouraging exhibitors to set up a contest with the following angle: "All women fall into two general classifications from a beauty-point-of-view. By analyzing the attractions of two beautiful stars of 'The Two Mrs. Carrolls,' contestant should be able to evaluate her own charms at the same time." Another press book exploits the title of Irving Rapper's *Deception* (1946) to sell make-up with the expert's claim that "Most beauty is a delightful deception." The "Exploitation" page of the press book for *In This Our Life* (1942) articulates connections between the different media—magazines, radio, cinema—and underlines the status of the star as an intertextual phenomenon with its headline: "Bette Davis Story in 'Ladies Home Journal' Cues Campaign for Femme Business!" The story is about how Bette Davis manages to keep a career and hold a husband as well and is entitled "Could your Husband take it?"

The very familiarity and banality of such ploys should not blind us to the overwhelming intensity of the injunction to the female spectator-consumer to concern herself with her own appearance and position—an appearance which can only be fortified and assured through the purchase of a multiplicity of products. The woman's film as a genre, together with the massive extracinematic discursive apparatus, insure that what the woman is sold is a certain image of femininity. There is a sense in which the woman's film is not much to look at—the non-style or zero degree style of films of the genre has frequently been noted. It is as though there were a condensation of the eroticism of the image onto the figure of the woman—the female star proffered to the female spectator for her imitation (and often this took place in extracinematic discourses—outside the context of particular filmic narratives which frequently de-eroticized the female protagonist). The process underlines the tautological nature of the woman's role as consumer: she is the subject of a transaction in which her own commodification is ultimately the object. As Rachel Bowlby points out, "Seducer and seduced, possessor and possessed of one another, women and commodities flaunt their images at one another in an amorous regard which both extends and reinforces the classical picture of the young girl gazing into the mirror in love with herself."[26] Even when consumerism concerns the objects of the space which she inhabits, its tendency is essentially narcissistic. For all consumerism involves the idea of self-image (perhaps this is why the woman is the prototype of the consumer.)

Consumerism requires a transformation in modes of perception. Looking and buying are closely linked. Wolfgang Schivelbusch argues that the development of the department store in the latter half of the 19th century profoundly altered the notion of the attractiveness of an item, which now ". . . results from the totality of *all* the goods assembled in the salesroom. . . . In the department store, the goods achieve more of their character *as* goods—their appearance as items of exchange value; one might say that their 'commodity-esthetic' aspect becomes ever more dominant."[27] At the cinema, the consumer glance hovers over the surface of the image, isolating details which may be entirely peripheral in relation to the narrative. It is a fixating, obsessive gaze which wanders in and out of the narrative and has a more intimate relation with space—the space of rooms and of bodies—than with the temporal dimension. It is as though there were another text laid over the first—a text with an altogether different mode of address—so that the film becomes something of a palimpsest. In this other text, the desire to possess displaces comprehension as the dominant mechanism of reading. Jameson refers to ". . . a quasi-material 'feeling tone' which floats above the narrative but is only intermittently realized by it: the sense of density in family novels, for instance, or the 'epic' rhythms of the earth or of great movements of 'history' in the various sagas can be seen as so many commodities towards whose consumption the narratives are little more than means, their essential materiality then being confirmed and embodied in the movie music that accompanies their screen versions."[28] It is the sense of the film as spectacle, and desirable in its very appeal to the eye, which is consumed in the viewing.

Walter Benjamin, in his essay "The Work of Art in the Age of Mechanical Reproduction" refers to a possible history of the modes of human sense perception and to the decay of the aura which characterizes contemporary perception. This decay is associated with the development of mass culture and with the "desire of contemporary masses to bring things 'closer' spatially and humanly, which is just as ardent as their bent toward overcoming the uniqueness of every reality by accepting its reproduction."[29] The processes of reproduction and commodification have in common the leveling of differences between things and the promotion of their abstract comparability through the medium of money. Schivelbusch uses Benjamin's claim to argue that the development of the railroad as a new form of transportation and of the circulation of commodities functions in much the same way—bringing geographical locations closer and annihilating the uniqueness of the outlying regions. His argument ultimately links together the railroad, the cinema, the department store, and modernized traffic patterns in the constitution of what he calls, "panoramic perception": "In the filmic perception—i.e., the perception of *montage*, the juxtaposition of the most disparate images into one unit—the new reality of annihilated in-between spaces finds its clearest expression: the film brings things closer to the viewer as well as closer together."[30]

Benjamin's conceptualization of the opposition between the effect of the aura and that of mechanical reproduction is expressed in the spatial terms of "distance" and "closeness." The aura attached to natural objects is "the unique phenomenon of a distance, however close it may be."[31] And the logic of the consumer's relation to the commodity annihilates this distance: "Every day the urge grows stronger to get hold of an object at very close range by way of its likeness, its reproduction."[32] It is not accidental that the logic of consumerism and mechanical reproduction corresponds to a logic of perception attributed to the female spectator whose non-fetishistic gaze maintains a dangerous intimacy with the image. For the woman, as outlined above, is positioned as the preeminent consumer. What we tend to define, since Marx, as commodity fetishism is in fact more accurately situated as a form of narcissism. Fetishism, in the Freudian paradigm, is a phallic defense which allows the subject to distance himself from the object of desire (or, more precisely, its implications in relation to castration) through the overvaluation of a mediating substitute object. Narcissism confounds the differentiation between subject and object and is one of the few psychical mechanisms Freud associates specifically with female desire.[33]

Having and appearing are closely intertwined in the woman's purportedly narcissistic relation to the commodity. Commodification presupposes that acutely self-conscious relation to the body which is attributed to femininity. The effective operation of the commodity system requires the breakdown of the body into parts—nails, hair, skin, breath—each one of which can constantly be improved through the purchase of a commodity. As Stuart Ewen points out, in relation to this "commodity self," "Each position of the body was to be viewed critically, as a *potential* bauble in a successful assemblage."[34] The ideological effect of commodity logic on a large scale is therefore the deflection of any dissatisfaction with one's life or any critique of the social system onto an intensified concern with a body which is in some way guaranteed to be at fault.[35] The body becomes increasingly *the* stake of late capitalism. *Having* the commodified object—and the initial distance and distinction it presupposes—is displaced by *appearing*, producing a strange constriction of the gap between consumer and commodity. The form of affect which embodies this constriction is also an affect aligned with the feminine—empathy. As Benjamin points out, "If the soul of the commodity which Marx occasionally mentions in jest existed, it would be the most empathetic ever encountered in the realm of souls, for it would have to see in everyone the buyer in whose hand and house it wants to nestle."[36] Commodity and consumer share the same attributes—appeal to the eye and an empathetic relation to the other—and become indistinguishable. Just as the category of "youth" has been expropriated by the commodity system and, as Guy Debord maintains, "is in no way the property of those who are now young,"[37] "femininity" as a category is not the possession of women—it is not necessarily something we should strive to reclaim. The feminine position has

Quar. Rev. of Film & Video, Vol. 11, pp. 35–60
Reprints available directly from the publisher
Photocopying permitted by license only

Harwood Academic Publishers, 1989
Printed in the United States of America

The Queen Christina Tie-Ups: Convergence of Show Window and Screen

Jane Gaines

At the turn of the century, the motion picture was not the only medium "commanding the eye."[1] Among the other features of modern life which trained the view and oriented the aspiration, one complementary and analogous medium stands out: the department store window. If early department store customers were an "audience for a spectacle of sales," as one current history of advertising describes them, motion picture spectators could easily be seen as "casual shoppers."[2]

A new consumer culture literature has reminded us of the similarities between the motion picture theater and the palatial department store. The architectural resemblances are certain, but also in both one sees the phenomenon of "riches" proffered vicariously to the public, spread as wide vista or panorama. Neither institution escaped public censure for dangling temptations before the masses. In France, the new *grands magasins* were "dens of iniquity"[3] and in the U.S., the great stores which swallowed small trades were called "monsters," "vultures," and "producers of crime, sorrow, and disgrace."[4] A recent historical study of the Bon Marché takes as its premise that the department store was "a creation of bourgeois culture both capturing and threatening many things that culture stood for,"[5] an analysis which easily serves as a description of popular cinema. Both institutions enshrined principles of capitalist enterprise and have continued to thrive because of the contradictions of capitalism, offering product-fantasies as compensations for deficiencies in social life, and, in a way, openly encouraging social behavior which challenges bourgeois codes. The interchangeability of the institutions directs us toward a history and theory of what Nick Browne has referred to as the "consuming subject."[6]

Cinema-going was analogous to the browsing-without-obligation-to-buy pioneered by the turn-of-the-century department store, where one could, with no offense to the merchant, enter to peruse the goods, exercising a kind of visual connoisseurship, and leave without purchase. Like the department store, the popular cinema extended the visual access to luxury goods made possible by the 18th-century industrial revolution. Here the distinction between visual access and actual possession is important. While some historians of consumer culture argue

JANE GAINES is Assistant Professor of English at Duke University, Durham, North Carolina 27706. She is currently working on a book on the history of commodity tie-ups and product licensing in motion pictures and television.

that the significant factor which marks the revolution in consumption accompanying the industrial revolution was the extension to wage earners of the ability to buy, the question of whether manufactured goods were actually affordable for this new group of spenders still remains.[7] What is certain is that purchasing became a public instead of a private transaction, and luxury commodities, once cloistered in the back of the store for the restricted purview of an elite clientele, were moved forward for all to see.[8] Contrary to the claim that cornucopian department stores evidenced equal purchase opportunity, Michael Schudson argues, in reference to the late 19th century, that "Luxury was not democratized so much as made markedly more visible, more public, and often more articulate—through advertising—than it had been before."[9]

The history of the bourgeois department store and the principles of merchandising reveal a connection between consumer product advertising and the department store as luxury accommodation which is based as much or more on the refinement of a visual "commodity aesthetic"[10] as on the sophistication of the verbal rhetorical "appeal." The first and most significant step in the transformation of the unshaped, unarticulated dry good, whether bolt of cloth or plank of wood, is its fashioning into a ready-made object-image. Significantly, in Marxist theory, this is the notorious moment when the human labor which endows the commodity with value is expended without the knowledge of the laborer, which becomes the basis for surplus value extracted, and which provides the foundation for capitalist society.[11] The raw material which becomes object-image is able to imply a use, inspire a want, connote a social context, and even suggest a purchase scenario. Semiotically, it is no mystery why the fashioned good, culturally inscribed as it is, would be more articulate than the unfashioned. Retail merchandising history, however, finds the discovery of the eloquence or the "self-advertising properties" of goods a significant breakthrough. Testimony to this is the way F. W. Woolworth is remembered among the great American merchants for having genuinely democratized the act of buying by limiting his stock to every conceivable trinket that could sell for five or ten cents, and for his insistence that since the goods could "speak for themselves," he didn't need to advertise them by any other means.[12] The goods themselves, then, if put on public view, evidenced their own promise and generated their own appeals.

The self-advertising properties of commodities were further enhanced by the installation of an amplifying medium which rivals the cinema in its tendency toward transparency—glass. Originally a scarce and valued commodity itself, glass serviced the dissemination of luxury ideas by its apparent dissolution of old distinctions which seemed to signal the breakdown of social as well as architectural boundaries. Huge sheets of plate glass set into the lighter cast-iron frames of the new 19th-century department store edifice opened up life-size street-view display space, which came to be known in the U.S. as the merchant's "show window."[13] If the impetus behind window display was to bring luxury closer to the masses, to familiarize it, and to represent the world of the middle-class parlor as an extension of the space of everyday life, the cinema would improve upon this in the drawing-room comedies and melodramas first produced in the teens.

The silent-film parlor drama could effortlessly achieve another aspiration of store window design: the elevation of merchandise above the status of merchant's stock. The turn-of-the-century window, analogous with the mail-order catalogue, was stuffed with rows and towers of boxed or canned goods or "trimmed" with star- and heart-shaped designs produced by pinning handkerchiefs or linens to cheese- cloth backgrounds. The "top-dressed window," as it was called, looked as though the back supply room had been moved into the storefront and was, in fact, arranged to testify to the abudance of the stock.[14] This stocky style had the disadvantage of turning from busy pattern into flat wallpaper on the city street; further, since such "mixed display" included goods for every potential customer, everyone's need was anticipated but no one's need was dramatized.[15] The principle of massed goods left "need" unarticulated and "audience" undifferentiated. Thus, the style which su- perseded massed display worked because empty space opened up possibilities for directing the eye and reorienting the body of the passerby. When Selfridge's in London began to isolate goods in their windows around 1909, crowds gathered.[16]

"Open display," as the new style was called, indicated the discovery of new spatial planes in the window. The "top-dressed" window had been oriented exclu- sively toward the front pane; now the backdrop was integrated and utilized to serve the ends of a new "realism" in window dressing. But whereas in cinema history screen "realism" pertains to the sharpening of the image in depth, window realism meant a "softening" of the hard edge of the commodity, which would be gradually achieved in a number of ways. Hard floodlighting was replaced by a new design which featured and complemented the goods;[17] the show card and price tag, once prominent, diminished in size and finally disappeared.[18] Painted scenes modified the merchant's shelf and counter top connotations of the window and suggested real-life uses for commodities. After a short period of interest in "lifelikeness," however, display aesthetics, first in Europe and finally in the U.S., abandoned the attempt to replicate the natural, and around 1926, windows began to aspire to the modernism of European poster art.[19]

The show window, too close in proximity to the brazenness of commerce, too box-like, too clearly artificial, was not, finally, the best medium for representing a luxury world continuous with the familiar world of the potential customer. Stand- ing before the show window, the "consuming subject" does not experience "reality confusion," mistaking representations for perceptions—as, sitting immobilized, he or she would in the motion picture theater.[20] Ironically, in show window visual rhetoric, based on the verifiability of the claims made by the "thing itself," the real thing announces that it is not, after all, the final referent. The mannequin, for instance, has historically "stood for" but has not tried to resemble the human body. The turn-of-the-century male mannequin stood like a "scarecrow" in the suit- maker's window; the Art Deco papier-mâché female mannequin could be identi- fied, *seen* as nothing more than a mute, stiff, signifier for "woman."[21] The goods themselves, in the context of the window, have historically stood for something else, for who would want them in their display form?

This "standing-in" capacity is more perceptible in the display medium as it also is in those modernist works of art which make known their conditions of construc- tion. The show window, however, is different from high art modernism in that the display medium comes to this knowledge *because of* the commercial origins which it does not transcend and cannot disown. Because of the impossibility of passing itself off as "the real," because it featured goods out of their "normal" places and reveled in this discontinuity, display has had an affinity with surrealism. But while

Cocteau, Dali, Duchamp, and Breton were interested in the subversive possibilities of the window, using commercial display to mock commercialism, the surrealist impulse could be easily turned into a publicity-stunt "attention grabber" designed to stop the shopper.[22] Modernist display worked because its "attractive sudden-ness" could reach out to snag the hurrying shopper;[23] the surrealist shock aesthetic arrested the view of the mobile shopper, and redirected his or her path. As the professional publication *Display World* described it in 1934, the goal of window design was to create and reenact desire and decision *at the door of the shop.*[24]

In the 1930s, the heyday of motion picture commodity tie-ups, cooperative advertising arrangements between merchant and exhibitor helped to coordinate desire and decision so that they occurred at the same moment and in the proximity of department store or motion picture theater, local florist shop, hardware store, or car dealer showroom.[25] Before television, the relationship between entertainment program and commodity appears to have been relatively loose, with local exhibitor and merchant each scrambling for a free ride on the other's publicity vehicle. During this period, it is difficult to distinguish the commodity host from the commodity parasite because of the complexity of the mutual benefit arrangements. Certainly there are premonitions of television here in the use of the consumer product to conceal economic relations. Local merchants received such visually enticing display material as eight-by-ten glossies, and star cut-outs, which saved them the expense of the services of a window dresser, and exhibitors borrowed the merchant's store window which, like a "twenty-four hour poster," extended adver-tising exposure past the hours when the theater doors were open and beyond the actual run of a particular picture.[26] These arrangements were especially vital to the sale of the motion picture commodity, which, in comparison with a pair of shoes or a box of soap flakes, has a relatively brief "shelf life."[27]

Motion picture theatrical advertising has historically worked against the perish-ability of its product by trying to turn the star into a cultural phenomenon, and it has accomplished this no more effectively than in the official star fashion tie-up within which it is impossible to tell where promotion leaves off and spontaneous cultural response begins.[28] Star styles are also a moment in the commodification of culture where merchandising efforts are so intertwined that it is difficult to deter-mine whether the sales advantage accrues to motion picture or ladies' garment industry. While the woman's wear manufacturers and fashion retailers transformed ready-to-wear clothes into star imagery,[29] motion pictures multiplied the possi-bilities for product tie-ups as they became, in Charles Eckert's description, "living display windows . . . occupied by marvelous mannequins."[30]

The following considers the show window and screen analogy by offering a reading of an unlikely alliance. From the point of view of the studio publicist or the local exhibitor in 1933, MGM's *Queen Christina* (Rouben Mamoulian 1933) would offer numerous "opportunities" for tie-ups with a range of consumer products. But how easily does a film about a 17th-century monarch who wears trousers translate into retail merchandising ideas? What is the logic in producing a line of women's fashions to coordinate with a film featuring a star who reputedly hated clothes? This, then, is also about the dissemination of a visual aesthetic, its spread from screen to department store display, its tapering off from bold, arrogant design and combative statement to trendy accent, and its "comeback" as camp.

Queen Christina reigns as one of a very few lesbian classics which offer an uncompromised gift to the lesbian viewer—the enigmatic, androgynous Greta Garbo, playing the bisexual queen, bestows a meaningful kiss on her lady-in-waiting. Both straight and lesbian feminists have recalled and savored this moment, and relished the swaggering image of Garbo wearing pants tucked into high boots, sitting with one leg crossed over the other. This subculture classic, which has delighted gay males as well as lesbians, contains a heterosexual "cover" discourse, and here I will be interested in the way one discourse offers up a text for recuperation while another discourse seems to escape.[31] How, I want to ask, can a text be ideologically complicit and indigestible at the same time?

Pioneering work in gay and lesbian film studies has based a theory of reception on the observation that narrative codes and stylistic codes often part company. While the narrative holds to the "straight and narrow," style is free to meander.[32] One recent feminist analysis of *Queen Christina* sees narrative codes as overriding other codes in the film. For instance, the interpretation of the film as producing a negative judgment on Christina's masculinity, based on a reading of her exile as punishment, suggests that narrative codes are stronger than other codes, since they "win out in the end," so to speak.[33] Actually, *Queen Christina* should be a basic text in our study of the ascendancy of style and the power of subcultural reclamation since, based on the equivocation of the final shot of Garbo at the masthead, it is so often cited as a film which undeniably leaves all to the reader.[34] The inventive lesbian analysis of the film, which completely discounts Garbo's coupling with Antonio, the Ambassador of Spain (John Gilbert), takes license with the narrative, an exercise of the reading prerogative of the subcultural group.[35] Since Antonio is killed in a duel by another lover, Christina's jealous Minister of the Treasury, she can, in the end, be strong and alone, and decidedly lesbian.[36]

Queen Christina is easy reading for lesbians in comparison with other mainstream texts in which there is a good deal more imaginative embroidering to do to make the narrative come out in favor of women loving women. But what I want to suggest is that feminists should have been suspicious when *Queen Christina* yielded so easily to the lesbian reading, because there is more to this film than a kiss.[37] A hornet's nest of issues are raised when we look squarely at style.

Cinema semiotics has theorized the significance of nonrepresentational stylistics, with close attention to camera movement, cutting, and music, for instance, but the systematized study of costume style as cinematic language has, as yet, not been undertaken. Roland Barthes' elaborate work in *The Fashion System* awaits adaptation and application; Umberto Eco's semiotic theory, which could provide the basis for an understanding of style in dress as a linguistic phenomenon, still needs to be tested.[38] Recent work on oppositional style, such as Dick Hebdige's *Subculture*, has investigated the signifying potency of the most ordinary item of apparel, and, with its shift of interest to appropriation and reclamation, has laid the groundwork for theorizing dress as *parole*. Hebdige's analysis of the affinity between subcultures and fashion suggests that style works as a vehicle of expression for oppressed groups because it is simultaneously "celebrated" as fashion news and "reviled" as social scourge in the wider culture.[39] Style in dress is thought to be obvious and self-evident, yet the subcultural uses of style may be completely misunderstood by the larger group. For the marginal group, then, style in dress is a rhetoric in another register.

In gay culture's appreciation of Hollywood design and the appropriation of its codes, we find a clue to the function of oppositional sensibilities. Although Holly-wood production and publicity organs in the thirties and forties stimulated the public anticipation of extravagant screen costumes and especially encouraged women to attend the movies just to see the stars wear spectacular gowns, the actual articulation of costume elements was still subject to restraining rules. Gay culture interest in the star icon and her costume to the exclusion of everything else in the production is a hint that costume, in its superfluity, can seriously exceed the bounds of convention. Realism, as the rule governing acting style, makeup, and sets as well as costume, had its stipulations and constraints; considering the more flamboyant Hollywood designers in retrospect, what strikes us now is the way they worked between realism and untempered expressionism. Let me suggest how far they could deviate.

Costuming, like color and decor, can burst out as pure spectacle. Historically, classical realist cinema has set parameters for the kind of spectacle which threat-ened to interfere with the ultimate goal of this cinema—storytelling.[40] Within the limits of realism, narrative can rationalize spectacle, even as genre can motivate the spectacular. Thus, the musical or the historical period piece justifies elaborate costuming as either fantasy or authenticity. The melodrama with its wider range of expressivity can accommodate costume as spectacle more easily than the western or the war film, for example. But especially in the melodrama we see the way costum-ing, like other potentially spectacular devices, is subordinated to narrative require-ments. Within the bounds of narrative economy and cinematic realism as well as the limits of social acceptability, Gilbert Adrian's costuming for Garbo sowed the seeds of an oppositional aesthetic. Where it ought to have been eclipsed, it was seen; where it should have been quiet and subdued, it was flagrant.[41] This oppositional aesthetic actually works for subcultural groups because of the notion of cinematic transparency which encourages the spectatorial practice of seeing through clothes as cinematic signifiers. Considering this, we could divide an audience into social groups based on those who do *not* see costume (as costume), but see characters dressed appropriately, and "camp" enthusiasts—those who see nothing else![42] Adrian's star designing is characterized by surprise and visual unpredictability, ironic humor, and often direct commentary on the actress, a kind of visual cattiness.

Adrian's whimsical design for design's sake often conflicted, then, with the costumer's code as it adhered to laws of continuity cinema. According to this code, the dress is not to compete with the dramatic content, and to do so is to become an intruder in the narrative. As designer Howard Shoup explained the relation of costume to narrative:

A design could not be so outstanding that it could kill a scene or make the audience gasp. There had to be a reason to have a spectacular dress.[43]

If the genre or the narrative did not provide sufficient rationale for Adrian's visual experiments, he would use the star personality as justification. Or, he would justify extravagant design as requisite to believable performance. The function of the fussiest attention to authenticity, in, for instance, the design of undergarments, would be to help actor or actress to realize the role. Adrian would go beyond adding extra yards of pleated, ruffled silk organdy to Garbo's underskirts in *Camille* (1936), designing to "fire her imagination."[44]

Figure 1. *"Puritan austerity and medieval torture,"* Queen Christina, 1933.

Figure 2.   Adrian's tunic and trousers for Garbo, Queen Christina, 1933.

The *Queen Christina* designs, fuel for Garbo's imagination and spectacular distractions, are also Adrian's sartorial essay on sexuality and power. The stiff, sharp, white collar and cuffs, juxtaposed with black velvet, are signifiers of Puritan austerity and medieval torture; the collar which slices the head off at the neck carries connotations of the guillotine and the rack. In the severity of the shapes is an echo of the iconography of old world monarchical power: parchment, armor, sword, and throne (Figure 1). The predominant motif brings the white geometric absolutes into contact with the soft black velvet. This combination is repeated in the tunic and trousers cavalier outfit first seen in the film and in the full-length state robe Christina wears in the scene in which she signs Antonio's passport out of Sweden (Figure 2). Following classical narrative costuming rules which stipulate that dress should construct a coherent character, Adrian's gowns for Christina are interrelated, with the play on stiffness as opposed to velvety softness threaded through the costumes, translating the Garbo androgyny into an unnerving aesthetic.

The costuming in *Queen Christina* is slightly disturbing for another reason. The costume which announces its status as accouterment is also somewhat disconcerting because it says too much about the constructed nature of symbolic power. Clifford Geertz has observed that well-established monarchies have developed elaborate disguises for their need to "anthropomorphize" power by locating it in the body of the sovereign.[45] But the ritual enactments and the paraphernalia of rule—the royal garb and the regalia of state—are often so pronounced as symbolic expression that they give it all away. Royal vestments and ornaments point to the symbolic use of power all the while they are putting it into effect. Or, as Geertz theorizes this:

The very thing that the elaborate mystique of court ceremonial is supposed to conceal—that majesty is made, not born—is demonstrated by it.[46]

Queen Christina further emphasizes the ritual aspect of the assumption of power in the incorporation of so many scenes which involve putting on and taking off the signs of state—Christina's coronation and her abdication in which she removes the crown from her own head. The robing and the disrobing also suggest something of the relation between the body of the monarch and the bodies of her subjects; and *Queen Christina* shows us the old world sovereign as embodiment of the law and guarantee of her subjects' existence. Reproductive chance dramatically demonstrates to monarchical subjects the connection between their fates and the biological body of the ruler. For her subjects, Christina's body is the battleground in a nationalistic effort to maintain racial purity, and their animosity toward the Spanish Ambassador is based on the threat the dark-complexioned Southerner poses to their snow white race. Vicariously dressing and undressing the monarch, following the parade of courtiers into the queen's bedroom, viewers—like the queen's subjects in history—gain some fantasy control over their fate.

The two dressing scenes in *Queen Christina* also organize the connection between clothes and gender roles and set up the homosexual/heterosexual flip-flop. In the first instance, Christina is dressed as a man by her valet; in the second, she is outfitted as a female by three women. In one way, this is a test of the prohibition; in another it is a kind of titillation. Garbo the female actress can be helped into stiff

Figure 3.   *"Power located in the body of the sovereign,"* Queen Christina, 1933.

boots by a man when Christina the character is indifferent to heterosexuality; the same female actress can be assisted in her toilette by women when the character has apparently renounced her lesbianism. The actress/character dichotomy allows extra play on sexual preference, and this is the basis of the subcultural claim on the film, as I will show.

Adrian's unsettling combinations also feed our curiosity about Christina's sexuality. What makes our discoveries particularly delicious is the aesthetic use of history—density of detail signifies density of desire and depth of passion. Sue Harper, in her analysis of decor and costume in Gainsborough period pictures produced in the 1940s, observes how history is a "source of sensual pleasures" in the screen adaptation of historical novels:

The affective, spectacular aspects of mise-en-scène are foregrounded, to produce a vision of "history" as a country where only feelings reside, not socio-political conflicts.[47]

History, the depository of emotion, provides the alibi, the license to act as voyeurs in respect to our own past.

The narrative cliché—woman's sexual maturation from tomboy to full heterosexual female, signified through her renunciation of pants in favor of dresses—is lightly parodied in the juxtaposition of the bedroom scene in the inn with Christina's second dressing scene. The shot of Christina and Antonio stretched before the fire dissolves into a close-up of her reflection in her dressing table mirror, an abrupt shift from male admiration to self-surveillance.[48] Here, she is assisted in her preparations by two chambermaids and a matron, while Aage, her valet, sulks in the corner, registering in his posture a history of male disdain for feminine fussiness and absorption in self-presentation. But while all the primping-for-the-male-suitor clichés are present in this scene, it is also preparation for an official court function for which Christina is fortified with an armor-like vestment trimmed with wide bands woven of silver threads, cut steel, and square diamonds (Figure 3). (Again, I find that the alternation of vulnerability and impenetrability in the costume strains.) The private audience scene with Antonio following the court appearance justifies Christina's change from the high-necked ceremonial robe into the off-the-shoulder low-cut dark velvet gown similar to the ball dresses she would later wear in *Camille* and *Anna Karenina* (1935). The low cut here is motivated by the narrative requirement that she produce a coin from her bodice, but the gesture calls up connotations of narcissism and homosexuality, since the token Christina treasures is Swedish national currency bearing her own image, and the sentiment attached to it is derived from the fact that it is the "tip" Antonio has given her in her guise as a young man. After this scene, Christina does not continue to dress as seductress, and her next appearance requires her to stand against the people and her minister's objection to her affair with the Spanish ambassador. For this dramatic purpose, she is made imposing and authoritative in a full-length black fur-trimmed coat and matching hat with horizontal braiding running the full length of the coat and parallel on both sleeves. Christina is again costumed in trousers as she rides to the rendezvous with Antonio, and for the final scene she wears the velvet traveling dress which recapitulates the major costume strands in the film—the tunic cut, the velvet softness, and the wide-brimmed hat (Figure 4).

The costume discourse in *Queen Christina* serves the cause of ambiguity rather than narrative clarification, and thus undermines any case for seeing the film as sharply divided into pre- and post-heterosexual initiation. Certainly, the costume pattern makes it difficult to see *Queen Christina* as lesbianism in the service of heterosexuality, à la *Emmanuelle* (1974) in which the young woman is sexually awakened from an infantile lesbianism by real love with a man. But, finally, based on the story the costume tells, it is equally difficult to see the film's enigmas as neatly resolved for lesbianism. Adrian's designs fashion the full erotic continuum for Garbo. In conventional romantic cuts, she is heterosexual; in drag, mirroring Antonio's gestures and dress, she articulates male homosexuality (Figure 5); in her male dress courtship of the skirted Ebba, Garbo acts out a butch-femme lesbian fantasy. At her abdication, stripped of her ermine robe and crown and draped in white, she takes on an asexual ethereality.

"Fashion," says Elizabeth Wilson in *Adorned in Dreams*, "is obsessed with gender, defines and redefines the gender boundary."[49] Women are attracted to the vagaries of fashion precisely because they suspect that there is an analogy between gender shift and clothes change. In the vicissitudes of fashion, and particularly in its inconsistency in relation to gender, women (who have historically been bound by garment) may see something of the arbitrary connection between selves and

Figure 4. *"Adrian's designs fashion the full erotic continuum,"* Queen Christina, *1933.*

socially assigned places. Sandra Gilbert, in "Costumes of the Mind," finds this clothing metaphor employed by female modernist and postmodernist writers. In comparison with male modernists, their female contemporaries tend to conceive of costuming as a metaphor for the way women assume multiple selves as they would "dress up," putting on and taking off articles of clothing.[50] I would liken this acute feminist awareness of social metamorphoses to camp, the sensibility trained in and through the necessity of "putting on," to pass as straight. Passing, says John Babuscio, ". . . leads to heightened awareness and appreciation of disguise, impersonation. . ."[51] And further, this practice explains the gay enthusiasm for actors and actresses who, in performances which seem to acknowledge sexual role-play, appear to understand the dynamics of passing. Thus, Garbo's Christina, who, like Virginia Woolf's Orlando, seems to have an entire "wardrobe of male and female selves,"[52] has articulated the possibilities of sexual fluidity for fifty years of gay and lesbian readership. In addition to the strategy of sex-role fluctuation, the history of homosexuality suggests that gay males and lesbians have found refuge in an indeterminate sexuality. Slipping out of the vestments of state into cavalier garb, out of the court where, as she says, "everything is constrained," Christina's escape from Sweden may position her in an indeterminate category, analogous to the gender-free third sex.[53] For women, third-sex neutrality has a special appeal, says Gilbert, because it enables them to "stand ironically outside subordination, like customers in a dress shop refusing to buy uncomfortable clothes."[54]

Gilbert contrasts this feminist ironic attitude toward dress with the seriousness of male modernist writers such as James Joyce, T. S. Eliot, and D. H. Lawrence, who use costume metaphorically to stand for "falsehood" in opposition to the "truth of the self." In their work, disaster and "misrule" is coincident with such social reversals as men wearing women's clothing. The worst nightmare these writers can imagine is a world in which gender is indeterminate, and Gilbert interprets this counter use of costume as a resoundingly conservative preference for clear-cut social divisions and hierarchies.[55] Male privilege, finally, is deeply invested in the *confirmation* of gender identity.[56]

In "Redressing the 'Natural'," where she makes the case for the existence of a temporary transvestite subgenre, Chris Straayer suggests that the political test of a film featuring gender disguise rests on notions of right and wrong in gender and costume coordination. The thinly disguised character with ill-fitting garb who may deceive his or her suitors (but does not fool the audience) broadly announces the impropriety or incorrectness of a "real" man in feminine dress or vice versa. Straayer finds that correcting the gender mix-up within the narrative is a smug collusion with the mainstream audience's view of the "obvious naturalness" of gender and costume coordination.[57] The film which does *not* correct gender mistakes by putting costumes on the appropriate bodies, she says, imagines more radical possibilities such as blurred gender distinctions and same-sex eroticism.[58] By this measure, gender mix-ups which are left unfixed are more progressive than *Tootsie* (1982), for example. *Tootsie*, within the tradition of the comedy which flirts with homoeroticism, would be finally reactionary in Straayer's analysis because Michael Dorsey's masquerade as Dorothy is ceremoniously shown to be false.

The putting on and taking off possibilities of the character in drag, then, can serve to establish gender categories finally and irreversibly. The narrative featuring

Figure 5.   Indeterminate gender as misrule, Queen Christina, *1933.*

gender disguise goes upriver against conventional morality in order to resolve gender ambiguity correctly. The conservative appeal of gender dissemblance is in the safeness and assurance that beneath the disguise there is evidence of the real and true—the actual sex—and that one sex or the other will eventually be confirmed. This is "recourse to the real" with a vengeance. Truth, or accuracy in sexuality, rests on the assumption that anatomical sex has its verifiably correct practice and preference. Gender dissemblance, then, does not necessarily spread the gender confusion which feminists would like to encourage.

The narrative correction of Christina's wrong dress would suggest that the Garbo vehicle belongs in Straayer's reactionary category. Again, the serious discrepancy between anatomy and clothing as it evokes images of disorder, confusion, and mockery of justice, suggests that *Queen Christina* is yet another costume-drama of misrule, which illustrates male fears. Because Sweden is ruled by a woman in male dress, everything else is reversed—Christina's whole kingdom is upside down. In this topsy-turvy world, a woman dominates and men acquiesce, the child queen chastens adult men for crying at her coronation, and, grown, she scolds them for their "petulance." In state affairs, the queen declares the end of costly and debilitating wars, against the protests of her all-male parliament. A Sweden dedicated to peace is dangerously out of step with the rest of Europe, which is an "armed camp," her Chancellor warns. With Christina's abdication in favor of her war hero cousin Charles, Sweden is "righted."

Clearly, the reactionary reading of *Queen Christina* in the above vein benefits from an interpretation of the disrobing scene at the inn as the moment of gender rectification. The actual "discovery" of Christina's true gender, however, is so subtly handled that it still remains ambiguous, and the image is once more able to evade gender resolution. Antonio and Christina, apparently two gentlemen who have arranged to share the only respectable room for the night, begin to undress, preparing to sleep together. Antonio (Gilbert) sits down on the bed and begins to remove his jacket and sword. The camera alternates between the two, and at her turn, before she removes her jacket, Christina reaches inside it in a gesture that could be read as either that she fears that her secondary sex characteristics will give her away or that she is merely hesitating before she unfastens her coat. The three shots following offer only a little more clarification. The medium close-up of Christina with head bowed, framed to emphasize the shape beneath her loose white blouse, is paired with Antonio's reaction shot, coded "male look," but the following long shot from behind Antonio showing Christina full length, backlit by the fire, suggests something else. While Christina's downcast eyes and coy pose suggest "modesty," the conventional posture of female nudity unveiled, she stands yet fully dressed as a man.[59]

If any filmgoers in 1934 were left with the smallest doubt about the thoroughness of Garbo's transformation, the promotional material for the film cleared up all ambiguities. In a campaign organized around Garbo's reunion with John Gilbert, the one-liners interpreted the film for the public: "She Was Crowned King of Sweden . . . Lived and Ruled as a Man . . . But Surrendered to Love!" and "They Crowned Her King of Sweden . . . But Within Her Frigid Heart a Tempestuous Lover Found an Amorous, Glamourous Woman."[60] *Screen Romances* carried the story version and Macy's Cinema Shop merchandised suits, coats, and hostess gowns (but not trousers) "inspired" by the film.[61] In her analysis of Hollywood pressbooks from the teens through the forties, Diane Waldman has shown how publicity campaigns aggressively applauded traditional roles for women. Gimmicks, stunts, contests, and commodity tie-up arrangements, she found, "serve to foreground preferred readings and to constrain oppositional ones. . . ."[62] Although an unusual stunt might encourage an oppositional reading and underwrite a nontraditional point of view, overwhelmingly, the publicity directed at women "channelled their interests toward romance, marriage and consumption."[63] Thus, such tie-ups and cooperative advertising as the window display connecting *Queen Christina* with a half-price flatware sale secured the meanings of the film and resolved its fluctuations for heterosexuality (Figure 6).

Consumer culture thrives on heterosexuality and its institutions by taking its cues from heterosexual "norms" and by deriving its iconography from heterosexual "ideals." Read from the standpoint of mutual merchandising benefits and chances for product tie-ups, Christina's transformation and the scene at the inn signify her initiation into consumer desire. Whereas Christina is austere and self-denying in her solitary state, heterosexuality *makes her want things.* She awakens from sleeping with a man sensitized to the properties of the objects in the room. Touching the spinning wheel, grasping the raw wool, crawling over the soft bed, rubbing her face against the pillow case, hugging the bedpost, examining the religious icon on the wall, she associates her fantasies with the tactility of the contents of the room. Christina the character "memorizes" the room; Greta Garbo the star invests household products with glamour, and the local exhibitor counts product tie-ups. The candelabra inspires a vision of the elegantly set table—opportunities to feature goblets, china, silver service, linen napkins and tablecloths. Garbo nuzzles fresh grapes Antonio has brought with him from Spain—opportunities for tie-ups with the local grocer!

Heavily brocaded and richly carved furnishings, glossy floors, and gilt-framed oil portraits of aristocratic figures, the mise-en-scène of the historical pageant picture, fanned the consumption aspirations of the homemaker. First, the richly appointed motion picture, like the department store interior, would help to make those not acquainted with opulence more comfortable with it, and often in consumer culture rhetoric this has been encouraged with the analogy between the housewife and the queen. Rachel Bowlby describes the turn-of-the-century department store as both the housewife's "escape from dull domesticity" and a "second home" where she was made to feel pampered.[64] Here, the strategy for encouraging buying was to eliminate the distinctions between the home and the store:

This combination would also tend to reinforce the potential for crossing the boundaries between looking and having: the real home could be made more of a fantasy place where she felt at home and enjoyed the democratic privilege of being treated like royalty.[65]

If the shopper had little to spend, like Theodore Dreiser's unemployed Carrie Meeber, she might feel the "drag of desire," the importuning of the goods she could not afford. Like Carrie, she might sense the judgment against her humbleness from the "fine ladies who elbowed and ignored her, brushing past in utter disregard of her presence" or from the sales clerks who snubbed customers whose dress and demeanor did not evidence "respectability."[66] Motion pictures, then, might be seen

Figure 6.   Tie-up with a half-price flatware sale, Queen Christina, *1933.*

as the medium which mingled consumption aspirations with the woman's reverie but in the darkness and the privacy of the theater where no class insult could disturb the vision. *Queen Christina* would offer uninterrupted access to the unbounded opulence as well as the absolute power of monarchy, for the female viewer, an abundant and favorite fantasy. Historical fiction for women, whether in the form of juvenile books, magazine serials, or motion pictures, has been fond of the lives of such European queens as Elizabeth I and Mary of Scotland. Although the romance with a courtier often figures in this fiction, the fascination for women would also have to do with the court intrigue, the wild adventure, the fabulous wealth, and the unchallenged position these monarchs would have enjoyed, often represented in such fictional accounts as the fame and adoration of their people. In these narratives, the queen's virtue is rewarded not by the love of a man (these men are often impediments) but by the devotion of her subjects. Fantasies of unlimited resources expressed not in terms of territorial acquisition, but in the iconography of the coronation ceremony and other royal pageantry and ritual, as well as fantasies of the unlimited devotion of millions of people, may be in strong competition with the fantasy of heterosexual romance.

As it sets up the narrative enigma as the "kingdom or the man," *Queen Christina* would seem to be posing a choice which is improbable for a queen and impossible for an ordinary woman. The "kingdom or the man" dilemma is impossible for the woman without inherited family wealth for whom the only way to the "kingdom" of a stable, comfortable home has historically been through the male earner. Actually, for the working-class woman, as well as for most middle-class women, "kingdom" and "man" are synonymous. Although the publicity material for *Queen Christina* consistently refers to the character as "modern" and the story as "modernized," this does not mean that Christina's dilemma has to do with rectifying her independent character with romance. The dichotomy organizing this film is not career or marriage. The kingdom or romantic love antithesis, rather, diverts the viewer from a more important set of oppositions which neatly deliver the viewer to consumption in the interests of higher American ideals. Christina abdicates because, she says, "I am a Queen . . . yes, but first I am a woman. . ." and, further, she "longs to be a human being" rather than a symbol. She cannot understand why her subjects do not want her to have what they have for themselves. What is it that Christina's subjects have that she does not have? They are private citizens and they are ordinary—they are free to feel, to choose whom they will love. Christina longs to be just like everyone else, and in her yearning, she *is* the same as everyone else.

Consistently, the film opposes the traditions which Christina questions with the concepts of "freedom" and "individual rights." She complains that, as a queen, she is an "obstruction." From the point of view of American republicanism, monarchy is weighty and constrains individuals. In its popular "liberty or death" form, this ideology expresses its animosity toward monarchy in terms of personal choice. But there is a peculiar inconsistency in the American attitude which is enamored of coronations and weddings, the iconographic trappings of royalty, but claims a superiority to those European states which have retained symbolic monarchies. Something of this ambivalence is fastened on the monarch in exile who brings the conflict between commoner and blueblood into focus. The marketing campaign for *Queen Christina* uses this fascination with the exiled monarch in an article entitled "When Christina Gave Up Her Throne the Whole World Thought Her Mad":

What happens to a regent who either abdicates from his throne willingly or is violently deposed therefrom? The last twenty-five years have seen so many kingdoms turned into republics that the spectacle of a king or a queen in exile is no longer startling to us: we accept with equanimity the fact that the ex-Spanish ruler lives in France, the ex-German one in Holland, the ex-Cuban in upper New York State, and on indefinitely. But three hundred years ago the deposition or abdication of a monarch was a fantastic and horrible event which upset a whole nation and even a whole continent. . .[67]

These republican sympathies, as I have pointed out, are rearranged in *Queen Christina*, or rather scrambled to certain ideological ends. The abdication of the monarch as represented in *Queen Christina* does not put a continent in political turmoil, but is rather understood as the turmoil of a woman in love. In this version of monarchy unseated, it is not the people who suffer because of divine right rule, it is the queen herself. Christina is modern, then, because she renounces the Old World absolute power of the monarch and embraces the republican "freedoms." It is in the weak moment of Christina's longing to be a human being that the discourses of motion picture promotion, in league with consumer culture, find their chord of recognition. Christina's lament lends itself to the fan magazine and studio publicity version of the star who, in spite of wide fame, unapproachability, and spectacular wealth, wants to be like everybody else. To want no more than to be a woman, when one is actually a queen, is to *want no more than anybody else has.* Fans who have less are flattered that the queen or star who apparently has so much more wants what is within reach of the ordinary woman—the love of a man. It is not far from here to: "If the star only wants what the ordinary woman has, why shouldn't the ordinary woman want what the star has?" Christina, after all, only wants to return to the room at the inn, and her dream—two people alone on an island in the Mediterranean, a vision of political isolationism and bourgeois marriage. After having had a kingdom, this is not asking for much. The lives of the great monarchs, like the lives of the Hollywood stars, are made comprehensible, and something of their allure is placed within economic reach of many wage earners.

Star styles, then, functioned like the original inspiration behind F. W. Woolworth's five and dime—to offer the opportunity to spend and to acquire in affordable terms. Hence, the screen style "elastic imitation" which may have made only an oblique reference to the screen original.[68] But here I have argued that Adrian's screen originals were subversions of gender assumptions which have historically played best, that is for the richest response, to an audience attuned to camp, and further, I have found in them the tinge of misogyny—one of the telling marks of gay male camp (Figures 7 and 8).

Hebdige has argued that the commodification of such cultural expression detoxifies it by making it widely intelligible. Or, he says, "as soon as original innovations which signify 'subculture' are translated into commodities and made generally available, they become 'frozen'." Produced for general consumption, objects which once signified opposition "become codified, made comprehensible, rendered at once, public property and profitable merchandise."[69] The *Queen Christina* costumes are a problem in this regard. As part of the motion picture mise-en-scène, they are already commodified culture, hence "frozen" in Hebdige's term. But are they completely comprehensible to the mainstream audience? Richard Dyer has argued that the patterns of dress and decor and other nonrepresentational signs may carry the "unspeakable,"[70] and here I have suggested that the *Queen Christina* costuming as a whole represents to the gay audience an erotic range and diversity which the wider audience would not be able to decipher. Individual costumes are unsettling combinations of shape and texture with disturbing implications (notably the guillotine effect) when considered as commentary on the female body. While some of this designing may be seen as an erotic exchange with both gay male and lesbian audiences, some of the extremity can also be attributed to Adrian's attempt to create designs that would resist further commodification. In their own attempt to semiotically "jam" the fashion waves by complicating a costume message so that it could not be easily copied, designers in this period experimented with strange cuts and unconventional fabric combinations. Because manufacturers could not make money copying the intricate designs which were too pronounced for most women to "carry off," the woman's fashion trade dubbed Hollywood costumes "spinach."[71] But it has always seemed to me as I have considered the copies, those mass-produced, diluted versions that the designers abhorred, that the designers often had the last sartorial word. The *Queen Christina*-"inspired" styles, for instance,

Figure 7.   The "tinge of misogyny" in Queen Christina-*inspired styles.*

carry over a flicker of Christina's unconventionality which is uneasy in the form of a filmy bouffant-sleeved evening gown. In translation, the austere white collar on black motif suggests the unfortunate prudery of the spinster stereotype, costuming for Arthur Miller's *The Crucible* rather than elegant party clothes or smart street wear. The bows do not soften the hard edges of the look—they are conspicuously attached to the dresses in a too obvious attempt to "feminize" the lines. The wide white collar chokes when it is up; and down, it rests on the mannequin's shoulders like a large doily on a Victorian side table. Adrian's fashion advice to women was often quoted in fan magazines, but his warning to them about copying Greta Garbo seems almost threatening:

. . .remember, when you are following Garbo, that you are taking dynamite sticks into your hands. You can be blown into the realms of the ridiculous by lack of knowledge as to how to handle the things you most admire.[72]

My final question is about the status of the sign as it shifts from context to context. What, for instance, happens to the meaning of the *Queen Christina* costumes when they cease to be mise-en-scène and find another existence as window dressing in hopes of having still another existence as everyday clothing? Very little theoretical

Figure 8. *"The display case magnifies aesthetic disturbance in the design,"* Queen Christina, *1933.*

work has been done to help us with this semiotic issue, but some consideration of recontextualization provides a starting point. Here, I would mention Tony Bennett's work on James Bond as a "mobile" signifier.[73] As a "portable" signifier, the image of Bond can be inserted in an unlimited number of texts, and it even, says Bennett, in reference to everyday linguistic uses and consumer product forms, "reaches ultimately beyond the world of texts."[74] But the show window and the screen, as I have shown, are sometimes analogous, or they converge as display media because of their similar commercial and aesthetic aspirations. Is the window, then, as special adjacent context, completely "beyond" the motion picture narrative? Does the cultural text, whether fiction film or realist novel, suddenly stop at the final frame or the last page, or does the circulating imagery of such promotional texts as the consumer product or advertising poster suggest one long, chain-like text? Or are the various semiotic offshoots like textual emissaries which spin off into new contexts but which always owe something to the narrative which spawned them?[75]

As I have suggested here, an adjacent promotional context such as the show window has a shaping function as it directs viewers to interpretations, or as it justifies the transformation of iconography into product and serves as a bridge between soft screen aesthetic and hard consumer good. The image, whether star body or fashion accouterment, skips from context to context, its movement hastened by commercial reproduction, so that it is difficult to see commodification as "freezing" culture as Hebdige has argued. Instead, commodification seems to facilitate circulation by multiplying the number of possible contexts. The show window, then, is not the deep freeze of culture but a medium of circulation. Neither does commercialization completely neutralize culture once and for all. Since, as I noted at the outset, the window can either feature or expose the motivations of commodity culture, depending upon the use of this commercial space, context does not correlate predictably with meaning. Although the china display claims the *Queen Christina* iconography for consumer culture goals, the dress displays do not necessarily recuperate the Christina style for woman as consumer of the glamour effect. Adrian's costumes do not translate logically into conventionally "pretty" dresses, and the display case magnifies the aesthetic disturbances in the design. But note that it is only in the most recent recontextualization— this feminist essay on *Queen Christina*—that the window can clearly be seen as accentuating a misogynist aesthetics. Here the headless and armless torsos, and the empty shoes like missing feet, can be understood as dismemberment of the female form, and can be made to protest the uses of woman in the image world as well as in everyday life.

NOTES

Stills from the Academy of Motion Picture Arts and Sciences, Doheny Library, with permission from MGM entertainment.

1. Stuart and Elizabeth Ewen, in *Channels of Desire* (New York: McGraw-Hill, 1982), p. 32, describe newspapers' use of bold typeface and illustration around 1890 as an attempt to "command the eyes and minds of their readership."

2. Michael Schudson, *Advertising, the Uneasy Persuasion* (New York: Basic Books, 1984), p. 150. See Judith Barry's feminist videotape *Casual Shopper* for a critical examination of the contemporary advertising aesthetic, heterosexual romance, and shopping mall culture.

3. M. B. Miller, *The Bon Marché: Bourgeois Culture and the Department Store* (London: Allen & Unwin, 1981), p. 197.

4. Schudson, p. 150.

5. Miller, P. 236.

6. Nick Browne, "The Political Economy of the Television (Super) Text," *Quarterly Review of Film Studies* 9, no. 3 (Summer 1984): 181.

7. For the argument that the revolution in consumption was related to increased wages in the 18th century, see Neil McKendrick, "The Consumer Revolution of Eighteenth-Century England," in *The Birth of a Consumer Society*, Neil McKendrick, John Brewer, and J. H. Plumb (Bloomington: Indiana University Press, 1982). Schudson, p. 151, takes issue with Daniel Boorstin, who he thinks has overestimated workers' incomes in the 19th century in *The Americans: The Democratic Experience* (New York: Random House, 1975). In a review of Stuart Ewen's *Captains of Consciousness* (New York: McGraw-Hill, 1976), Daniel Horowitz notes that this significant study of consumption makes optimistic assumptions about workers' pay in the early 20th century ("Consumption, Capitalism, and Culture," *Reviews in American History* 6 [September 1978]). Jeanne Allen, in "The Film Viewer as Consumer," *Quarterly Review of Film Studies* 5, no. 4 (Fall 1980), is also skeptical of the idea that moviegoing in the early years of the cinema in the U.S. was the result of the "democratization" of consumption.

8. Boorstin, pp. 101–108.

9. Schudson, p. 151.

10. David Chaney, "The Department Store as a Cultural Form," *Theory, Culture & Society* 1, no. 3 (1983): 27.

11. For full explication of this, see Karl Marx, *Capital*, vol. 1, trans. Ben Fowkes (New York: Random House, 1977).

12. Boorstin, p. 114.

13. Ibid. P. 325.

14. R. Harman, "Progress in the Art of Window Display," in *The Art of Window Display*, ed. H. Ashford Down (London: Sir Isaac Pitman, 1931), p. 16.

15. Leonard Marcus, *The American Store Window* (New York: Whitney Library, 1978), p. 18.

16. Harman, p. 16.

17. Ibid., p. 41.

18. Marcus, p. 18.

19. Ibid., p. 5.

20. For the theory of the way the cinema viewer mistakes representations for perceptions, see Christian Metz, "The Fiction Film and Its Spectator," *New Literary History* 8, no. 1 (Autumn 1976).

21. Marcus, p. 35.

22. Ibid., pp. 33–36.

23. Holbrook Jackson, "Modernist Window Display," in *The Art of Window Display*, p. 52.

24. William Whiting, "Window Salesmanship," *Display World* 25, no. 1 (July 1934): 22.

25. John F. Barry and Epes W. Sargent, *Building Theatre Patronage* (New York: Chalmers, 1927), p. 247.

26. Ibid., p. 134.

27. Joe Morella and Edward Epstein, *Those Great Movie Ads* (New York: Arlington House, 1972), p. 109.

28. On the marketing of star fashions see Charles Eckert, "The Carole Lombard in Macy's Window," *Quarterly Review of Film Studies* 3, no. 1 (Winter 1978); Charlotte Cornelia Herzog and Jane Marie Gaines, " 'Puffed Sleeves Before Tea Time': Joan Crawford, Adrian and Women Audiences," *Wide Angle* 6, no. 4 (Spring 1985): 24–33.

29. Mary Ann Doane, in "The Economy of Desire: The Commodity Form in/of the Cinema," in this issue, describes the way the tie-up "disperses the fascination of the cinema onto a multiplicity of products."

30. Eckert, p. 4.

31. Molly Haskell, in *From Reverence to Rape* (New York: Holt, Rinehart, and Winston, 1973), p. 132, suggests that Christina's affair with Antonio is a "cover romance."

32. Edith Becker, Michelle Citron, Julia Lesage, and B. Ruby Rich, "Lesbians and Film," in *Jump Cut*, ed. Peter Steven (New York: Praeger, 1985), p. 301, say that often "the burden of proof for a lesbian analysis depends upon the interpretation of style." Their example is the lesbian star Alla Nazimova's production of the silent film *Salome* (1928).

33. Rebecca Bell-Metereau, in *Hollywood Androgyny* (New York: Columbia, 1985), p. 77, says, "Historical films like *Queen Christina* are problematic for they posit that women such as Christina do exist but do not survive as such. The masculine woman who is truly brave, gifted, and iron-willed is beyond the comprehension of society or any one man. Therefore, she is not allowed to live happily ever after, a situation which is quite true to life." Bell-Metereau here subscribes to an obtuse feminism which cannot imagine the lesbian analysis in which Christina "escapes" from a constraining society to live "happily ever after" without a man.

34. Raymond Durgnat and John Kobal in *Greta Garbo* (London: Dutton, 1965), p. 87, quote Simone de Beauvoir's reference to this scene: "Garbo's visage has a kind of emptiness into which anything could be projected." Richard Dyer, in *Stars* (London: British Film Institute, 1981), p. 63, refers to the well-known story that director Rouben Mamoulian told Garbo to do absolutely nothing for this shot. It is interesting to note that before the incursion of reader-response criticism into film theory, the assumption underlying close analysis seemed to be that some shots encouraged the viewer to "read" more into them than others, as though the reader's part in the construction of meaning was by invitation only.

35. See, for instance, Chris Straayer, "*Personal Best*: Lesbian/Feminist Audience," *Jump Cut*, no. 29 (February 1984); Elizabeth Ellsworth, "The Power of Interpretive Communities: Feminist Appropriations of *Personal Best*," paper delivered at Society for Cinema Studies Conference, University of Wisconsin–Madison, March 1984.

36. For illustrations of how lesbians have "rewritten" popular cinema, see Claire Whitaker, "Hollywood

Transformed: Interview with Lesbian Viewers," in Steven, pp. 106–118. One of Whitaker's interviewees, "Gladys," an Afro-American, interprets the later film version of Queen Christina's life: "When Liv Ullman played Queen Christina of Sweden in *The Abdication* [1974], in the end Hollywood had her fall in love with the Peter Finch character, which I'm sure she never did. I think she went to her grave having sex with women."

37. Thanks to Susan Willis for this insight and to Alex Wilson for helping to tease more out of this film. The important reference to the kiss is in Caroline Sheldon, "Lesbians and Film: Some Thoughts," in *Gays in Film*, ed. Richard Dyer (New York: Zoetrope, 1984), p. 17. It is interesting that Sheldon refers to Ebba as Christina's "chambermaid," and although the lover seems to have a ministering function, her status is quite clearly that of aristocratic lady-in-waiting.

38. Roland Barthes, *The Fashion System*, trans. Matthew Ward and Richard Howard (New York: Hill and Wang, 1983); Umberto Eco, *A Theory of Semiotics* (Bloomington: Indiana University Press, 1976).

39. Dick Hebdige, *Subculture* (London: Methuen, 1979), p. 93.

40. See Steve Neale, *Cinema and Technology: Image, Sound, Color* (Bloomington: Indiana University Press, 1985), pp. 145–151, for an analogous discussion of color.

41. David Bordwell in *The Classical Hollywood Cinema: Film Style and Mode of Production to 1960*, David Bordwell, Janet Staiger, and Kristin Thompson (New York: Columbia University Press, 1985), pp. 19–21, discusses this phenomenon as the "pursuit of virtuosity for its own sake."

42. Jack Babuscio, in "Camp and the Gay Sensibility," in *Gays and Film*, ed. Richard Dyer (New York: New York Zoetrope, 1984), p. 43, describes the aesthetic function of camp as "an emphasis on sensuous surfaces, textures, imagery and the evocation of mood as stylistic devices—not simply because they are appropriate to the plot, but as fascinating in themselves." Richard Dyer, in "It's being so camp as keeps us going," *Body Politic* 11 (September 1977): 12, defines camp perception as "a way of prying the form of something away from its content, of revelling in the style while dismissing the content as trivial."

43. As quoted in Margaret Bailey, "Those Glorious Glamour Years (Seacaucus, N.J.: Citadel, 1982), p. 36.

44. Robert Riley, "Adrian," in *American Fashion*, ed. Sarah Tomerline Lee (New York: Quadrangle, 1975), p. 32.

45. Clifford Geertz, "Centers, Kings, and Charisma: Reflections on the Symbolics of Power," in *Rites of Power: Symbolism, Ritual, and Politics Since the Middle Ages*, ed. Sean Wilentz (Philadelphia: University of Pennsylvania Press, 1985), p. 15.

46. Geertz, p. 16.

47. Sue Harper, "Gainsborough: What's in a Costume," *Monthly Film Bulletin* 52, no. 621 (October 1985): 324.

48. For this theory of woman's self-surveillance, see John Berger, *Ways of Seeing* (London: Penguin, 1972), pp. 45–47.

49. Elizabeth Wilson, *Adorned in Dreams: Fashion and Modernity* (London: Virago, 1985), p. 41.

50. Sandra Gilbert, "Costumes of the Mind: Transvestism as Metaphor in Modern Literature," in *Writing and Sexual Difference*, ed. Elizabeth Abel (Chicago: University of Chicago Press, 1982), p. 206. Shoshana Felman, in "Rereading Femininity," *Yale French Studies*, no. 62 (1981): 28, finds a similar insight in Balzac's "The Girl With the Golden Eyes." The nymphet Paquita is unwilling to discriminate properly between her two lovers, Henri de Marsay and his sister the Marquise, on the basis of gender; Felman notes:

If it is clothes, the text seems to suggest, if it is clothes alone, i.e., a cultural sign, an institution, which determine our reading of the sexes, which determine masculine and feminine and insure sexual opposition as an orderly hierarchical polarity; if indeed clothes make the *man*—or the woman—, are not sex roles as such, inherently, but travesties?

51. Babuscio, p. 45. Esther Newton in *Mother Camp: Female Impersonators in America* (Chicago and London: University of Chicago Press, 1972), p. 109, discusses drag as synonymous with distancing, costuming, and theatricality in the gay male community. This section also includes one of the clearest explanations of how Garbo functions as "high camp."

52. Gilbert, p. 207.

53. Esther Newton in "The Mythic Mannish Lesbian: Radclyffe Hall the New Woman," *Signs* 9, no. 4 (Summer 1984): 568–570, discusses the ramifications of the third sex position in relation to Hall's character Stephen in *The Well of Loneliness*. Although Freud, Havelock Ellis, and Krafft-Ebbing

considered the third sex as a frustrated woman, unfortunately "trapped" between genders, Radclyffe Hall and contemporaries such as Gertrude Stein and Vita Sackville-West embraced the concept. Considering the history of this classification, it may be much more effective for feminists to embrace Joan Nestle's suggestion in "The Fem Question," in *Pleasure and Danger*, ed. Carol Vance (Boston and London: Routledge & Kegan Paul, 1984), pp. 235–236, that "Lesbians should be mistresses of discrepancies, knowing that resistance lies in the change of context."

54. Gilbert, p. 219.

55. Ibid., p. 195. Her best example here is the Nighttown section of Joyce's *Ulysses* where Leopold Bloom encounters Bella the whorehouse madam, who turns into Bello, a male, and in turn transforms Bloom into first a female and then a pig.

56. I see something of this tendency in Roland Barthes' famous description in "The Face of Garbo," in *Mythologies*, trans. Annette Lavers (New York: Hill and Wang, 1972), p. 56; reprinted in Gerald Mast and Marshall Cohen, eds. *Film Theory and Criticism*, 3d ed., (New York: Oxford, 1985). He is enamored with her gender elusiveness, but he would finally pin her down:

> Garbo offered to one's gaze a sort of platonic idea of the human creature, which explains why her face is almost sexually undefined, without however leaving one in doubt. It is true that this film (in which Queen Christina is by turns a woman and a young cavalier) lends itself to this lack of differentiation; but Garbo does not perform in it any feat of transvestism; she is always herself, and carries without pretence, under her crown or her wide-brimmed hats, the same snowy solitary face.

> Garbo, whose face is "almost sexually undefined," transcends gender and is raised above sexuality, but since she is always the same underneath, her costumes belie her true or authentic self. She may be alternately male or female, but, for Barthes as for her many other male admirers, the guise fortunately does not succeed.

57. Chris Straayer, "Redressing the 'Natural'," paper delivered at Ohio University Film Conference, Athens, Ohio (October 1984), p. 2.

58. Ibid., p. 10.

59. Charles Affron, in *Star Acting: Gish, Garbo, and Davis* (New York: E. P. Dutton, 1977), p. 179, would seem to be agreeing with this reading as he says:

> After she removes her jacket, the barest alteration of posture is only one step removed from the previous ambiguity, and is not at all conventionally feminine.

> But like Gilbert's male modernists and Roland Barthes, Affron wants some final confirmation of the connection between gender and "identity," and although he is interested in entertaining gender ambiguity, this is finally a serious matter; Garbo's complexity is "beyond travesty and role-playing." For an interesting contrast with this reading, see Betsy Erkkila, "Greta Garbo: Sailing Beyond the Frame," *Critical Inquiry* 11, no. 4 (June 1985): 609. Consistent with Erkkila's argument for seeing *Queen Christina* as Garbo's break with Hollywood as well as a renunciation of the romantic plot, the inn scene marks an "auto-erotic self-making as she consummates the erotic sequence alone on the bed."

60. *Queen Christina* pressbook, n.p., Academy of Motion Picture Arts and Sciences Library, hereafter AMPAS.

61. "Queen Christina," *Screen Romances* (February 1934): 11–20.

62. Diane Waldman, "From Midnight Shows to Marriage Vows," *Wide Angle* 6, no. 2 (1984): 42.

63. Waldman, p. 48.

64. Rachel Bowlby, *Just Looking: Consumer Culture in Dreiser, Gissing and Zola* (New York and London: Methuen, 1985), p. 4.

65. Ibid.

66. Theodore Dreiser, *Sister Carrie* (New York: Modern Library, 1932), p. 24.

67. *Queen Christina* pressbook, n.p., AMPAS.

68. Harper, p. 327.

69. Hebdige, p. 96.

70. Richard Dyer, *Social Values of Entertainment and Show Business*, unpublished dissertation, Centre for Contemporary Cultural Studies, Birmingham University (October 1972), p. 337.

71. Gladys Parker, "Don't Call It Spinach!" *Screen Guide* 4, no. 9 (January 1940): 30–31.

72. Gilbert Adrian, "The Garbo Girl Sways the Mode," *Screenland* 18, no. 3 (January 1929): 27.

73. Tony Bennett, "Text and Social Process: The Case of James Bond," *Screen Education* 41 (1982): 10.
74. Bennett, p. 3.
75. Bennett is most concerned with arguing that the original context does not fix the meaning once and for all, and even that an original form cannot be privileged or isolated from those texts which have become attached to it. I am in agreement with him, but here I am more interested in the relationship between the "incrustation," as Macherey calls these textual modifiers, and the text-as-rock (Pierre Macherey, interview in *Red Letters*, no. 5 [Summer 1977]: 7, as quoted in Bennett, p. 3).

Quar. Rev. of Film & Video, Vol. 11, pp. 61–83
Reprints available directly from the publisher
Photocopying permitted by license only

Harwood Academic Publishers, 1989
Printed in the United States of America

Sitcoms and Suburbs: Positioning the 1950s Homemaker

Mary Beth Haralovich

The suburban middle-class family sitcom of the 1950s and 1960s centered on the family ensemble and its homelife—breadwinner father, homemaker mother, and growing children placed within the domestic space of the suburban home. Structured within definitions of gender and the value of homelife for family cohesion, these sitcoms drew upon particular historical conditions for their realist representation of family relations and domestic space. In the 1950s, a historically specific social subjectivity of the middle-class homemaker was engaged by suburban housing, the consumer product industry, market research, and the lifestyle represented in popular "growing family" sitcoms such as *Father Knows Best* (1954–1963) and *Leave It to Beaver* (1957–1963). With the reluctant and forced exit of women from positions in skilled labor after World War II and during a period of rapid growth and concentration of business, the middle-class homemaker provided these institutions with a rationale for establishing the value of domestic architecture and consumer products for quality of life and the stability of the family.

The middle-class homemaker was an important basis of this social economy—so much so that it was necessary to define her in contradictions which held her in a limited social place. In her value to the economy, the homemaker was at once central and marginal.[1] She was marginal in that she was positioned within the home, constituting the value of her labor outside of the means of production. Yet she was also central to the economy in that her function as homemaker was the subject of consumer product design and marketing, the basis of an industry. She was promised psychic and social satisfaction for being contained within the private space of the home; and as a condition of being targeted, measured, and analyzed for the marketing and design of consumer products, she was promised leisure and freedom from housework.

These social and economic appeals to the American homemaker were addressed to the white middle class whom Stuart and Elizabeth Ewen have described as "the landed consumer" for whom "suburban homes were standardized parodies of independence, of leisure, and, most important of all, of the property that made the first two possible."[2] The working class is marginalized in and minorities are absent from these discourses and the social economy of consumption. An ideal white and middle-class homelife was a primary means of reconstituting and resocializing the

---

Mary Beth Haralovich teaches film and television history at the University of Arizona, Tucson, Arizona 85721. Her research has appeared in Wide Angle, Screen, Enclitic, *and* Explorations in Ethnic Studies.

American family after World War II. By defining access to property and home-ownership within the values of the conventionalized suburban family, women and minorities were guaranteed economic and social inequality. Just as suburban housing provided gender-specific domestic space and restrictive neighborhoods, consumer product design and market research directly addressed the class and gender of the targeted family member, the homemaker.

The relationship of television programming to the social formation is crucial to an understanding of television as a social practice. Graham Murdock and Peter Golding argue that media reproduce social relations under capital through "this persistent imagery of consumerism conceal[ing] and compensat[ing] for the persistence of radical inequalities in the distribution of wealth, work conditions and life chances." Stuart Hall has argued that the ideological effects of media fragment class into individuals, masking economic determinacy and replacing class and economic social relations with imaginary social relations.[3] The suburban family sitcom is dependent upon this displacement of economic determinations onto imaginary social relations which naturalize middle-class life.

Despite its adoption of historical conditions from the 1950s, the suburban family sitcom did not greatly proliferate until the late 1950s and early 1960s. While *Father Knows Best*, in 1954, marks the "beginning" of popular discussion of the realism of this program format, it was not until 1957 that *Leave It to Beaver* joined it on the schedule. In the late 1950s and early 1960s, the format multiplied, while the women's movement was seeking to release homemakers from this social and economic gender definition.[4] This "nostalgic" lag between the historical specificity of the social formation and the popularity of the suburban family sitcom on the prime-time schedule underscores its ability to mask social contradictions and to naturalize woman's place in the home.

The following is an analysis of a historical conjuncture in which institutions important to social and economic policies defined women as homemakers: suburban housing, the consumer product industry, and market research. *Father Knows Best* and *Leave It to Beaver* mediated this address to the homemaker through their representations of middle-class family life. They appropriated historically specific gender traits and a realist mise-en-scène of the home to create a comfortable, warm, and stable family environment. *Father Knows Best*, in fact, was applauded for realigning family gender roles, for making "polite, carefully middle-class, family-type entertainment, possibly the most non-controversial show on the air waves."[5]

I. "LOOKING THROUGH A ROSE-TINTED PICTURE WINDOW INTO YOUR OWN LIVING ROOM"

After four years on radio, *Father Knows Best* began the first of its six seasons on network television in 1954. This program about the family life of Jim and Margaret Anderson and their children, Betty (age 15), Bud (age 13), and Kathy (age 8), won the 1954 Sylvania Award for outstanding family entertainment. After one season the program was dropped by its sponsor for low ratings in audience polls. But more than twenty thousand letters from viewers protesting the program's cancellation attracted a new sponsor (the Scott Paper Company), and *Father Knows Best* was promptly reinstated in the prime-time schedule. It remained popular even after first-run production ended in 1960 when its star, Robert Young, decided to move on to other roles. Reruns of *Father Knows Best* were on prime-time for three more years.[6]

Contemporary writing on *Father Knows Best* cited as its appeal the way it rearranged the dynamics of family interaction in situation comedies. Instead of the slapstick and gag-oriented family sitcom with a "henpecked simpleton" as family patriarch (presumably programs like *The Life of Riley*), *Father Knows Best* concentrated instead on drawing humor from parents raising children to adulthood in suburban America. This prompted the *Saturday Evening Post* to praise the Andersons for being "a family that has surprising similarities to real people":

The parents . . . manage to ride through almost any family situation without violent injury to their dignity, and the three Anderson children are presented as decently behaved children who will probably turn into useful citizens.[7]

These "real people" are the white American suburban middle-class family, a social and economic arrangement which was valued as the cornerstone of the American social economy of the 1950s. The verisimilitude associated with *Father Knows Best* is derived not only from the traits and interactions of the middle-class family, but also from the placement of that family within the promises which suburban living and material goods held out for it. Even while the role of Jim Anderson was touted as probably "the first intelligent father permitted on radio or TV since they invented the thing,"[8] the role of Margaret Anderson in relation to the father and the family— as homemaker—was equally important to post-World War II attainment of quality family life, social stability, and economic growth.

Leave It to Beaver was not discussed as much or in the same terms as *Father Knows Best*. Its first run in prime-time television was from 1957 to 1963, overlapping the last years of *Father Knows Best*. Ward and June Cleaver raise two sons (Wally, 12; Theodore—the Beaver, 8) in a single-family suburban home which, in later seasons, adopted a nearly identical floor plan to that of the Andersons. Striving for verisimilitude, the stories were based on the "real life" experiences of the scriptwriters in raising their own children. "In recalling the mystifications that every adult experienced when he [*sic*] was a child, 'Leave It to Beaver' evokes a humorous and pleasurably nostalgic glow."[9]

Like *Father Knows Best*, *Leave It to Beaver* was constructed around an appeal to the entire family. The Andersons and the Cleavers are already assimilated into the comfortable environment and middle-class lifestyle which housing and consumer products sought to guarantee for certain American families. While the Andersons and the Cleavers are rarely (if ever) seen in the process of purchasing consumer products, family interactions are closely tied to the suburban home. The Andersons' Springfield and the Cleavers' Mayfield are ambiguous in their metropolitan identity as suburbs in that the presence of a major city nearby is unclear, yet the communities exhibit the characteristic homogeneity, domestic architecture, and separation of gender associated with suburban design.

Margaret Anderson and June Cleaver, in markedly different ways, are two representations of the contradictory definition of the homemaker in that they are simultaneously contained and liberated by domestic space. In their placement as homemakers, they represent the promises of the economic and social processes which established a limited social subjectivity for homemakers in the 1950s. Yet there are substantial differences in the character traits of the two women, and these revolve around the degree to which each woman is contained within the domestic space of the home. As we shall see, June is more suppressed in the role of homemaker than is Margaret, with the result that June remains largely peripheral to the decision-making activities of family life.

Yet these middle-class homemakers lead a comfortable existence in comparison with television's working-class homemakers. In *Father Knows Best* and *Leave It to Beaver*, middle-class assimilation is displayed through deep focus photography which exhibits tasteful furnishings, tidy rooms, appliances, and gender-specific functional spaces—dens and workrooms for men, the "family space" of the kitchen for women. Margaret Anderson and June Cleaver have a lifestyle and domestic environment which is radically different from that of their working-class sister, Alice Kramden in *The Honeymooners*. The suburban home and consumer products have presumably liberated Margaret and June from the domestic drudgery which marks Alice's daily existence.

The middle-class suburban environment is comfortable, unlike the cramped and unpleasant space of the Kramden's New York City apartment. A major portion of the comedy of *The Honeymooners'* (1955–1956) working-class urban family is derived from Ralph and Alice Kramden's continual struggle with outmoded appliances, their lower-class taste, and the economic blocks to achieving an easy assimilation into the middle-class through homeownership and the acquisition of consumer goods. Ralph screams out of the apartment window to a neighbor to be quiet; the water pipe in the wall breaks, spraying plaster and water everywhere. The Kramden's refrigerator and stove predate the postwar era.

One reason for this comedy of mise-en-scène is that urban sitcoms such as *I Love Lucy* (1951–1957) and *The Honeymooners* tended to focus on physical comedy and gags generated by their central comic figures (Lucille Ball and Jackie Gleason) filmed or shot live on limited sets before studio audiences.[10] *Father Knows Best* and *Leave It to Beaver*, on the other hand, shifted the source of comedy to the ensemble of the nuclear family as it realigned the roles within the family. *Father Knows Best* was praised by the *Saturday Evening Post* for its "outright defiance" of "one of the more persistent cliches of television script-writing about the typical American family . . . the mother as the iron-fisted ruler of the nest, the father as a blustering chow-derhead and the children as being one sassy crack removed from juvenile delinquency." Similarly, *Cosmopolitan* cited the program for overturning television programming's "message . . . that the American father is a weak-willed, predicament-inclined clown [who is] saved from his doltishness by a beautiful and intelligent wife and his beautiful and intelligent children."[11]

Instead of building family comedy around slapstick, gags and clowning, the Andersons are the modern and model American suburban family, one whom—judging from contemporary articles about *Father Knows Best*—viewers recognized as themselves. The *Saturday Evening Post* quoted letters from viewers who praised the program for being one the entire family could enjoy and "even learn something from it." In *Cosmopolitan*, Eugene Rodney, the producer of *Father Knows Best*, identified the program's audience as the middle-class and middle-income family. "It's people in that bracket who watch us. They don't have juvenile delinquent problems. They are interested in family relations, allowances, boy and girl problems."[12] In 1959 *Good Housekeeping* reported that a viewer had written to the program to thank *Father Knows Best* for solving a family problem:

Last Monday my daughter and I had been squabbling all day. By evening we were both so mad that I went upstairs to our portable TV set, leaving her to watch alone in the living room. When you got through with us, we both felt like fools. We didn't even need to kiss and make up. You had done it for us. Thank you all very much.

Good Housekeeping commented fondly on the program's "lifelike mixture of humor, harassment, and sentiment that literally hits home with some 15 million mothers, fathers, sons, and daughters. Watching it is like looking through a rose-tinted picture window into your own living room." In this last season, *Father Knows Best* ranked as the sixth most popular show on television.[13]

The verisimilitude of *Father Knows Best* and *Leave It to Beaver* was substantially reinforced by being based at major movie studios (Columbia and Universal, respectively), with sets which were standing replications of suburban homes. The *Saturday Evening Post* described the living environment of *Father Knows Best*:

The set for the Anderson home is a $40,000 combination of illusion and reality. Its two floors, patio, driveway and garage sprawl over Columbia Pictures Stage 10. One room with interchangeable, wallpapered walls, can be made to look like any of the four different bedrooms. The kitchen is real, however. . . . If the script calls for a meal or a snack, Rodney insists that actual food be used. . . . "Don't give me too much food," [Young said] "Jim leaves quickly in this scene and we can't have fathers dashing off without cleaning their plates."

The home is a space not for comedy riffs and physical gags but for family cohesion, a guarantee that children can be raised in the image of their parents. In *Redesigning the American Dream*, Dolores Hayden describes suburban housing

as an architecture of gender, since houses provide settings for women and girls to be effective social status achievers, desirable sex objects, and skillful domestic servants, and for men and boys to be executive breadwinners, successful home handy men, and adept car mechanics.[14]

II. "THE HOME IS AN IMAGE . . . OF THE HOUSEHOLD AND OF THE HOUSEHOLD'S RELATION TO SOCIETY"

As social historians Gwendolyn Wright and Dolores Hayden have shown, housing development and design are fundamental cornerstones of social order. Hayden argues that "the house is an image . . . of the household, and of the household's relation to society."[15] The single-family detached suburban home was architecture for the family whose healthy life would be guaranteed by a nonurban environment, neighborhood stability, and separation of family functions by gender. The suburban middle-income family was the primary locus of this homogeneous social formation.

When President Harry Truman said at the 1948 White House Conference on Family Life that "children and dogs are as necessary to the welfare of this country as is Wall Street and the railroads," he spoke to the role of homeownership in transforming the postwar American economy. Government policies supported suburban development in a variety of ways. The 41,000 miles of limited-access highways authorized by the Federal-Aid Highway Act of 1956 contributed to the development of gender-specific space for the suburban family: commuter husbands and homemaker mothers. Housing starts became, and still continue to be, an important indicator of the well-being of the nation's economy. And equity in homeownership is considered to be a significant guarantee of economic security in the later years of life.[16]

But while the Housing Act of 1949 stated as its goal "a decent home and a suitable living environment for every American family," the Federal Housing Authority (FHA) was empowered with defining "neighborhood character." Hayden argues that the two national priorities of the postwar period—removing women from the paid labor force and building more housing—were conflated and tied to:

an architecture of home and neighborhood that celebrates a mid-nineteenth century ideal of separate spheres for women and men . . . characterized by segregation by age, race, and class that could not be so easily advertised.[17]

In order to establish neighborhood stability, homogeneity, harmony, and attractiveness, the FHA adopted several strategies. Zoning practices prevented multi-family dwellings and commercial uses of property. The FHA also chose not to support housing for minorities by adopting a policy called "red-lining," in which red lines were drawn on maps to identify the boundaries of changing or mixed neighborhoods. Since the value of housing in these neighborhoods was designated as low, loans to build and/or buy houses were considered bad risks. In addition, the FHA published a "Planning Profitable Neighborhoods" technical bulletin which gave advice to developers on how to concentrate on homogeneous markets for housing. The effect was to "green-line" suburban areas, promoting them by endorsing loans and development at the cost of creating urban ghettos for minorities.[18]

Wright discusses how the FHA went so far as to enter into restrictive or protective covenants to prevent racial mixing and "declining property values." She quotes the 1947 manual:

If a mixture of user groups is found to exist, it must be determined whether the mixture will render the neighborhood less desirable to present and prospective occupants. Protective covenants are essential to sound development of proposed residential areas, since they regulate the use of the land and provide a basis for the development of harmonious, attractive neighborhoods.

Despite the fact that the Supreme Court ruled in favor of the NAACP's case against restrictive covenants, the FHA accepted written and unwritten agreements in housing developments until 1968.[19]

The effect of these government policies was to create homogeneous and socially stable communities with racial, ethnic, and class barriers to entry. Wright describes "a definite sociological pattern to the household that moved out to the suburbs in the late 1940s and 1950s": the average age of adult suburbanites was 31 in 1950; few single, widowed, divorced and elderly; higher fertility rate than in the cities; 9 percent of suburban women worked, as compared to 27 percent in the population as a whole. According to Hayden, five groups were excluded from single-family housing through the social policies of the late 1940s: single white women; white elderly working and lower-class; minority men of all classes; minority women of all classes; and minority elderly.[20]

The suburban dream house underscored this homogeneous definition of the suburban family. Domestic architecture was designed to display class attributes and reinforce gender-specific functions of domestic space. Robert Woods Kennedy, an influential housing designer of the period, argued that the task of the housing architect was "to provide houses that helped his clients to indulge in status-conscious consumption . . . to display the housewife 'as a sexual being' . . . and to display the family's possessions 'as proper symbols of socio-economic class' claiming that [this] form of expression [was] essential to modern family life." In addition to the value of the home for class and sexual identity, suburban housing was also therapeutic for the family. As Hayden observes, "whoever speaks of housing must also speak of home; the word means both the physical space and the nurturing that takes place there."[21]

A popular design for the first floor of the home was the "open floor plan" which provided a whole living environment for the entire family. With few walls separating living, dining, and kitchen areas, space was open for family togetherness. This "activity area" would also allow children to be within sight and hearing of the mother. Father could have his own space in a den or workroom and a detached garage for his car, while mother might be attracted to a modern model kitchen with separate laundry room. Bedrooms were located in the "quiet zone," perhaps on the second floor at the head of a stairway, away from the main activities of the household. While children might have the private space of individual bedrooms, parents shared the "master bedroom," which was larger and sometimes equipped with walk-in closets and dressing areas.[22]

This housing design, built on a part of an acre of private property with a yard for children, allowed the postwar middle-class family to give their children a lifestyle which was not so commonly available during the Depression and World War II. This domestic haven provided the setting for the socialization of girls into women and boys into men, a place paid for by the labor of the breadwinner father and maintained by the labor of the homemaker mother. The homemaker, placed in the home by suburban development and housing design, was promised release from household drudgery and an aesthetically pleasing interior environment as the basis of the consumer product industry economy.

III. "LEISURE *CAN* TRANSFORM HER LIFE EVEN IF GOOD DESIGN CAN'T"

Like housing design and suburban development, the consumer product industry built its economy on defining the social class and self-identity of women as homemakers. But this industrial definition of the homemaker underwent significant changes during the 1950s as suburban housing proliferated to include the working class. Two significant shifts marked discussions among designers about the role of product design in social life. The first was in 1955 when, instead of focusing on practical problems, the Fifth Annual Design Conference at Aspen drew a record attendance to discuss theoretical and cultural aspects of design. Among the topics discussed were the role of design in making leisure enjoyable and the possibility that mass communications could permit consumer testing of products before the investment of major capital. Design was no longer simply a matter of aesthetically pleasing shapes, but "part and parcel of the intricate pattern of twentieth-century life." The second shift in discussions occurred in early 1958 when *Industrial Design* (a major trade journal in the field) published several lengthy articles on market research, which it called "a new discipline—sometimes helpful, sometimes threatening—that is slated to affect the entire design process."[23]

Other types of market research focused on the function of women as home-makers. Thus the economic responsibility for class status lay with the father while the mother was addressed through emotional connotations associated with home-making. Depth research looked into the psychic motivations of consumers and revealed, for example, that "women reacted with favorable emotions to [the] fresh, creamy surface of a newly opened shortening can." Ernest Dichter redesigned the Snowdrift shortening label with this emotional response in mind (Fig. 3). A swirl of shortening formed the letter "S" emerging from the can on a wooden spoon to further associations with traditional cooking. The s-shape integrated the name of the product with the emotional appeal of the texture of the shortening. Proof of these researcher deductions and, presumably, the typicality of homemaker emotions, was provided by IBM data-processing equipment which could handle large samples and quantify the results.[38]

Experimental research included projective techniques which would elicit unconscious responses to market situations, on the theory that consumers would impute to others their own feelings and motivations (Fig. 4). These techniques included word-association, cartoons in which word balloons were filled in, narrative projection in which a story was finished, role-playing, and group discussions. For example, women were shown the following two grocery lists and asked to describe the woman who used each list.

Shopping List I	*Shopping List II*
pound and a half of hamburger	pound and a half of hamburger
2 loaves of Wonder Bread	2 loaves of Wonder Bread
bunch of carrots	bunch of carrots
1 can Rumford's Baking Powder	1 can Rumford's Baking Powder
Nescafe instant coffee	1 lb. Maxwell House Coffee (Drip Ground)
2 cans Del Monte peaches	2 cans Del Monte peaches
5 lbs. potatoes	5 lbs. potatoes

Forty-eight percent of the women polled described the first shopper as lazy while only four percent attached that label to shopper #2. Women who considered instant coffee a trait of the lazy housewife were less likely to buy it, "indicating that personality image was a motive in buying choice."[39]

In perception tests, machines measured the speed with which a package could be identified and how much of the "message" of the design could be retained. Role-playing at shopping and group discussions at the Institute for Motivational Research's "Motivational Theater" were "akin to . . . 'psychodrama'" in that consumers would reveal product, class, and gender related emotions which researchers would elicit and study. These techniques "stimulate expression" by "putting oneself in another's position—or in one's own position under certain circumstances, like shopping or homemaking."[40]

Some designers complained that this application of science to design inhibited the creative process by substituting testable and quantifiable elements for aesthetics. In an address to the 1958 Aspen Conference, sociologist C. Wright Mills criticized designers for "bringing art, science and learning into a subordinate relation with the dominant institutions of the capitalist economy and the nationalist

Figure 3. (top) Ernest Dichter's redesign of the Snowdrift label: a swirl of shortening on a wooden spoon furthers associations with traditional cooking. Figure 4. (bottom) Perception studies measure the speed of package identification and reception of design message. Word associations reveal unconscious reactions to what subjects have seen below the perception threshold.

state." Mills' paper was considered to be "so pertinent to design problems today" that *Industrial Design* ran it in its entirety rather than publishing a synopsis of its major points, as it typically did with conference reports.[41]

Mills complained that design helped to blur the distinction between "human consciousness and material existence" by providing stereotypes of meaning. He argued that consumer products had become "the Fetish of human life" in the "virtual dominance of consumer culture." Mills attacked designers for promulgating "The Big Lie" of advertising and design, the notion that "we only give them what they want." He accused designers and advertisers of determining consumer wants and tastes, a procedure characteristic "of the current phase of capitalism in America . . . creat[ing] a panic for status, and hence a panic of self-evaluation, and . . . connect[ing] its relief with the consumption of specified commodities." While Mills did not specifically address the role of television, he did cite the importance of distribution in the postwar economy and "the need for the creation and maintenance of the national market and its monopolistic closure."[42]

V. TELEVISUAL LIFE IN SPRINGFIELD AND MAYFIELD

One way that television distributed knowledge about a social economy which positioned women as homemakers was through the suburban family sitcom. The signifying systems of these sitcoms invested in the social subjectivity of homemakers put forth by suburban development and the consumer product industry. In their representation of middle-class family life, series such as *Father Knows Best* and *Leave It to Beaver* mobilized the discourses of other social institutions. Realistic mise-en-scène and the character traits of family members naturalized middle-class homelife, masking the social and economic barriers to entry into that privileged domain.

The heterogeneity of class and gender which market research analyzed is not manifested in either *Father Knows Best* or *Leave It to Beaver*. The Andersons and the Cleavers would probably rank quite well in the Index of Social Position. Their neighborhoods have large and well-maintained homes; both families belong to country clubs. Jim Anderson is a well-respected insurance agent with his own agency (an occupation chosen because it would not tie him to an office). Ward Cleaver's work is ambiguous, but both men carry a briefcase and wear a suit and tie to work. They have the income which easily provides their families with roomy, comfortable, and pleasing surroundings and attractive clothing; their wives have no need to work outside the home. Both men are college-educated; the programs often discuss the children's future college education.

Father Knows Best and *Leave It to Beaver* rarely make direct reference to the social and economic means by which the families attained and maintain their middle-class status. Their difference from other classes is not a subject of these sitcoms. By effacing the separations of race, class, age, and gender which produced suburban neighborhoods, *Father Knows Best* and *Leave It to Beaver* naturalize the privilege of the middle-class. Yet there is one episode of *Leave It to Beaver* from the early 1960s which lays bare its assumptions about what constitutes a good neighborhood. In doing so, the episode suggests how narrowly the heterogeneity of social life came to be defined.

Wally and Beaver visit Wally's smart-aleck friend, Eddie Haskell, who has moved out of his family's home into a rooming house in what Beaver describes as a "crummy neighborhood." Unlike the design of suburban developments, this neighborhood has older, rambling two-story (or more) houses set close together. The door to one house is left ajar, paper debris is blown about by the wind and left on yards and front porches. Two men are working on an obviously older model car in the street, hood and trunk open, tire resting against the car; two garbage cans are on the sidewalks; an older man in sweater and hat walks along carrying a bag of groceries. On a front lawn, a rake leans against a bushel basket with leaves piled up; a large canvas-covered lawn swing sits on a front lawn; one house has a sign in the yard: "for sale by owner—to be moved."

Wally and Beaver are uneasy in this neighborhood, one which is obviously in transition and in which work activities are available for public view. But everyone visible is white. This is a rare example of a suburban sitcom's demarcation of good and bad neighborhoods. What is more typical is the assumption that the homes of the Andersons and the Cleavers are representative of the middle-class.

In different ways, the credit sequences which begin these programs suggest recurring aspects of suburban living. The opening of *Father Knows Best* begins with a long shot of the Anderson's two-story home, a fence separating the front lawn from the sidewalk, its landscape including trellises with vines and flowers. A cut to the interior entryway shows the family gathering together. In earlier seasons, Jim, wearing a suit and with hat in hand, prepares to leave for work. He looks at his watch; the grandfather clock to the left of the door shows the time as nearly 8:30 a.m. Margaret, wearing a blouse, sweater, and skirt, brings Jim his briefcase and kisses him good-bye. The three Anderson children giggle all in a row on the stairway leading up to the second-floor bedrooms. In later seasons, after the long shot of the house, the Anderson family gathers in the entryway to greet Jim as he returns from work. Margaret, wearing a dress too fancy for housework, kisses him at the doorway as the children cluster about them, uniting the family in the home.

The opening credits of *Leave It to Beaver* gradually evolved from an emphasis on the younger child to his placement within the neighborhood and then the family. The earliest episodes open with childlike etchings drawn in a wet concrete sidewalk. Middle seasons feature Beaver walking home along a street with single-family homes set back behind manicured, unfenced lawns. In later seasons, the Cleaver family is shown leaving their two-story home for a picnic trip: Ward carries the thermal cooler, June (in a dress, even for a picnic) carries the basket, and Wally and Beaver climb into the Cleavers' late model car. While *Father Knows Best* coheres around the family ensemble (Fig. 5), *Leave It to Beaver* de-centers the family around the younger child, whose rearing provides problems which the older child has either already surmounted or never had.

The narrative space of these programs is dominated by the domestic space of the home. *Father Knows Best* leaves the home environment much less often than *Leave It to Beaver*, which often focuses on Beaver at school. This placing of the family within the home contributes in large measure to the ability of these programs to "seem real." During the first season of *Leave It to Beaver*, the Cleavers' home was an older design rather than a suburban dream house. The kitchen was large and homey with glass and wood cabinets. The rooms were separated by walls and closed doors. By the 1960s, the Cleavers, like the Andersons, were living in the "open floor plan," a

Figure 5.   The suburban family sitcom in Father Knows Best *coheres around the family ensemble in the home.*

popular housing design of the 1950s. As you enter the homes, to your far left is the den, the private space of the father. To the right of the den is the stairway leading to the "quiet zone" of the bedrooms. To your right is the living room, visible through a wide and open entryway the size of two doors. Another wide doorway integrates the living room with the formal dining room. A swinging door separates the dining room from the kitchen. The deep focus cinematography typical of these sitcoms displays the expanse of living space in this "activity area."

While the Cleaver children share a bedroom, it is equipped with a private bathroom and a portable television set. Ward and June's bedroom is small with twin beds. Since it is not a site of narrative activity, which typically takes place in the boys' room or on the main floor of the home, the parents' bedroom is rarely seen. These two small bedrooms belie the scale of the house when it is seen in long shot.

The Anderson's home, for its part, makes more use of the potential of the bedrooms for narrative space. With four bedrooms, the Anderson home allows each of the children the luxury of his or her own room. Jim and Margaret's "master" bedroom, larger than those of their children, has twin beds separated by a nightstand and lamp, a walk-in closet, a dressing table, arm chairs, and a small alcove. In this design, the "master" bedroom is conceived as a private space for parents, but the Anderson children have easy access to their parents' bedroom. The Andersons, however, have only one bathroom. Betty has commented that when she gets married she will have three bathrooms because "there won't always be two of us."

The Andersons and the Cleavers also share similarities in the decor of their homes, displaying possessions in a comfortably unostentatious way. Immediately to the left of the Anderson's front door is a large, freestanding grandfather clock; to the right and directly across the room are built-in bookcases filled with hardbacks. In earlier seasons of *Leave It to Beaver*, the books (also hardbacks) were on shelves in the living room. Later, these books were relocated to Ward's study to line the many built-in bookshelves behind his desk.

The two families share similar taste in wall decorations and furnishings. Among the landscapes in heavy wood frames on the Cleavers' walls are pictures of sailing vessels and reproductions of "great art" such as "Pinkie" by Sir Thomas Lawrence. While the Andersons do not completely share the Cleavers' penchant for candelabra on the walls and tables, their walls are tastefully decorated with smaller landscapes. Curiously, neither house engages in the prominent display of family photographs.

The large living room in each home has a fireplace. There is plenty of room to walk around the furniture, which is overstuffed and comfortable or hard wood. The formal dining room in both homes includes a large wooden table and chairs which can seat six comfortably. It is here that the families have their evening meal. A sideboard or hutch displays dishes, soup tureens, and the like. The kitchen contains a smaller, more utilitarian set of table and chairs where breakfast is eaten. Small appliances such as a toaster, mixer, and electric coffeepot sit out on counters. A wall-mounted rack of paper towels is close to the sink. The Andersons' outdoor patio has a built-in brick oven, singed from use.

While both homes establish gender-specific areas for women and men, *Father Knows Best* is less repressive in its association of this space with familial roles. Both Jim Anderson and Ward Cleaver have dens; Ward is often shown doing ambiguous paperwork in his, the rows of hardbacks behind his desk suggesting his association with knowledge and mental work. June's forays into Ward's space tend to be brief, usually in search of his advice on how to handle the boys. As Ward works on papers, June sits in a corner chair sewing a button on Beaver's shirt. Ward's den is often the site of father-to-son talks. Its doorway is wide and open, revealing the cabinet-model television which Beaver occasionally watches. While Jim also has a den, it is much less often the site of narrative action, and its door is usually closed.

Workrooms and garages are also arenas for male activity, providing storage space for paint or lawn care equipment or a place to work on the car. The suburban homemaker does not have an equivalent private space. The family space of the kitchen, living room, and dining room is the woman's space. In typical episodes of *Leave It to Beaver*, June's encounters with family members generally take place in the kitchen, while Ward's tend to occur throughout the house. As her sons pass through her space, June is putting up paper towels, tossing a salad, unpacking groceries, or making meals. Margaret, having an older daughter, is often able to turn this family/woman space over to her. She is also more often placed within other domestic locations: the patio, the attic, the living room.

Both Margaret and June exemplify Robert Woods Kennedy's theory that housing design should display the housewife as a sexual being, but this is accomplished not so much through their positioning within domestic space as through costume. June's ubiquitous pearls, stockings and heels, and cinch-waisted dresses are amusing in their distinct contradiction to the realities of housework. While Margaret also wears dresses or skirts, she tends to be costumed in a more casual manner, and sometimes wears a smock when doing housework. Margaret is also occasionally seen in relatively sloppy clothes suitable for dirty work but marked as inappropriate to her status as a sexual being.

In one episode of *Father Knows Best*, Margaret is dressed in dungarees, sweatshirt, and loafers, her hair covered by a scarf as she scrubs paint from her youngest daughter, Kathy. When Betty witnesses this sight, she laughs, "If you aren't a glamourous picture!" As Jim arrives home early, Betty counsels Margaret, "You can't let father see you like this!" Betty takes over scrubbing and dressing Kathy while Margaret hurries off to change before Jim sees her. But Margaret is caught, embarrassed at not being dressed as a suburban object of desire. Jim goodnaturedly echoes Betty's comment: "If you aren't a glamourous picture!" He calms Margaret's minor distress at being seen by her husband in this departure from her usual toilette: "You know you always look great to me."

As this example shows, the agreement among Jim, Margaret, and Betty on the proper attire for the suburban homemaker indicates the success with which Betty has been socialized within the family. Yet even though both programs were created around "realistic" storylines of family life, the nurturing function of the home and the gender-specific roles of father and mother are handled very differently in *Father Knows Best* and *Leave It to Beaver*.

By 1960, Betty, whom Jim calls "Princess," had been counseled through adolescent dating and was shown to have "good sense" and maturity in her relations with boys. Well-kempt and well-dressed like her mother, Betty could easily substitute for Margaret in household tasks. In one episode, Jim and Margaret decide that their lives revolve too much around their children ("trapped," "like servants") and they try to spend a weekend away, leaving Betty in charge. While Betty handles the situation smoothly, Jim and Margaret are finally happier continuing their weekend at Cedar Lodge with all of the children along.

Bud, the son, participates in the excitement of discovery and self-definition outside of personal appearance. A normal boy in the process of becoming a man, he gets dirty at sports and tinkering with engines, replaces blown fuses, and cuts the grass. Unlike Betty, Bud has to be convinced that he can handle dating even though Jim counsels him that this awkward stage is normal and one which Jim himself has gone through.

Kathy (whose pet name is "Kitten"), in contrast to her older sister, possesses a tomboy persona and is interested in sports. By 1959, *Good Housekeeping* purred that

Kathy seems to have got the idea it might be more fun to appeal to a boy than to be one. At the rate she's going, it won't be long before [Jim and Margaret] are playing grandparents.[43]

Film and television writer Danny Peary was also pleased with Kathy's development, but for a very different reason: in the 1977 *Father Knows Best* "Reunion" show, Kathy was an unmarried gym teacher. Peary also felt that *Father Knows Best* was different from other suburban family sitcoms in its representation of women. "The three Anderson females . . . were intelligent, proud, and resourceful. Margaret was Jim's equal, loved and respected for her wisdom."[44] The traits which characterize Margaret in her equality are her patience, good humor, and easy confidence. Unlike Ward Cleaver, Jim is not immune to wifely banter.

In one episode, Jim overhears Betty and her friend, Armand, rehearsing a play, and assumes they are going to elope. Margaret has more faith in their daughter and good-naturedly tries to dissuade Jim from his anxiety: "Jim, when are you going to stop acting like a comic strip father?" In the same episode, Jim and Margaret play Scrabble, an activity which the episode suggests they do together often. "Dad's getting beat at Scrabble again," observes Bud. Kathy notices, "He's stuck with the 'Z' again." Margaret looks up Jim's Z-word in the dictionary, doubting its existence. Margaret is able to continually best Jim at this word game and Jim is willing to play despite certain defeat.

In contrast to this easy-going family with character traits which allow for many types of familial interaction, *Leave It to Beaver* tells another story about gender relations in the home. June does not share Margaret's status in intelligence. In a discussion of their sons' academic performances, June remarks: "We can't all be 'A' students, maybe the boys are like me." Ward responds: "No, they are *not* like you" and then catches himself up short. Nor does June share Margaret's witty and confident relationship with her husband. She typically defers to Ward's greater sense about raising their two sons. Wondering how to approach instances of boyish behavior, June positions herself firmly at a loss. She frequently asks, mystified, "Ward, did boys do this when you were their age?" And Ward always reassures June that whatever their sons are doing (brothers fighting, for example) is a normal stage of development of boys, imparting to her his superior social and familial knowledge. Like her sons, June acknowledges the need for Ward's guidance. Unlike Margaret, June is structured on the periphery of the socialization of her children, in the passive space of the home.

Ward, often a misogynist, encourages the boys to adopt his own cynical attitude toward their mother and women in general. In an early episode, Ward is replacing the plug on the toaster. He explains to Beaver that "your mother" always pulls it out by the cord instead of properly grabbing it by the plug. Beaver is impressed by Ward's knowledge of "'lectricity," to which Ward responds by positioning his knowledge as a condition of June's ineptness. "I know enough to stay about one jump ahead of your mother." Unlike *Father Knows Best*, *Leave It to Beaver* works to contain June's potential threat to patriarchal authority. When June asks why Beaver would appear to be unusually shy about meeting a girl, Ward wonders as well: "He doesn't know enough about life to be afraid of women."

In the episode in which Eddie Haskell moves out of the home, Ward agrees to support the Haskells and forbid their sons to visit Eddie's bachelor digs. As Ward telephones another father to ask him to do the same, June timidly asks (covering a bowl to be put in the refrigerator), "Ward, aren't you getting terribly involved?" Ward answers that if this were their son he would appreciate the support of other parents. June murmurs assent as Ward and June continue the process of defining June's function within the family in terms of passivity and deference.

While *Father Knows Best* and *Leave It to Beaver* position the role of the homemaker in family life quite differently, both women effortlessly maintain the domestic space of the family environment. In their representation of women's work in the home, these programs show the great ease and lack of drudgery with which Margaret and June keep their homes tidy and spotlessly clean. In any episode, these homemakers can be seen engaged in their daily housework. June prepares meals, waters plants, and dusts on a Saturday morning. She brings in groceries, wipes around the kitchen sink, and asks Wally to help her put away the vacuum cleaner (which she has not been shown using). Margaret prepares meals, does dishes, irons, and also waters plants. While June is often stationary in the kitchen or sewing in the living room, Margaret is usually moving from one room to another, in the process of ongoing domestic activity.

While one could argue that this lack of acknowledgment of the labor of home-making troubles the verisimilitude of these sitcoms, the realist mise-en-scène which includes consumer products suggests the means by which the comfortable environment of quality family life can be maintained. Margaret and June easily mediate the benefits promised by the consumer product industry. They are defi-nitely not women of leisure but women for whom housework is neither especially confining nor exclusively time-consuming.

The visible result of their partially visible labor is the constantly immaculate appearance of their homes and variously well-kempt family members. (The older children are more orderly because they are further along in the process of socializa-tion than the younger ones.) The "real time" to do piles of laundry or the daily preparation of balanced meals is a structured absence of the programs. The free time which appliances provide for Margaret and June is attested to by their continual good humor and the quality of their interactions with the family. Un-rushed and unpressured, Margaret and June are not so free from housework that they become idle and self-indulgent. They are well-positioned within the con-straints of domestic activity and the promises of the consumer product industry.

We have seen how the homemaker was positioned in the postwar consumer economy by institutions which were dependent on defining her social subjectivity within the domestic sphere. In the interests of family stability, suburban develop-ment and domestic architecture were designed with a particular definition of family economy in mind: a working father who could, alone, provide for the social and economic security of his family; a homemaker wife and mother who maintains the family's environment; children who grow up in neighborhoods undisturbed by heterogeneity of class, race, ethnicity, and age.

The limited address to the homemaker by the consumer product industry and market research is easily understood when taken within this context of homoge-neity in the social organization of the suburban family. Defined in terms of her homemaking function for the family and for the economy, her life could only be made easier by appliances. To ensure the display of her family's social status, experts assuaged any uncertainties she may have had about interior decor by designing with these problems in mind. By linking her identity as a shopper and homemaker to class attributes, the base of the consumer economy was broadened, her deepest emotions and insecurities tapped and transferred to consumer product design.

The representation of suburban family life in *Father Knows Best* and *Leave It to Beaver* also circulated social knowledge which linked the class and gender identities of homemakers. Realist mise-en-scène drew upon housing architecture and consumer products in order to ground family narratives within the domestic space of the middle-class home. The contribution of the television homemaker to harmonious family life was underscored by the ease with which she negotiated her place in the domestic arena.

This brief social history has placed one television format—the suburban family sitcom—within the historical context from which it drew its conventions, its codes of realism, and its definitions of family life. Yet we must also ask about resistances to this social subjectivity by recognizing the heterogeneity of the social formation. For example, in the late 1950s and 1960s, when the suburban family sitcom proliferated on prime-time television, the women's movement was resisting these institutional imperatives, exposing the social and economic inequalities on which they were based.[45]

Oppositional positions point to the inability of institutions to completely conceal the social and economic determinations of subjectivity. But the durability of the suburban family sitcom indicates the degree of institutional as well as popular support for ideologies which naturalize class and gender identities. Continuing exploration of the relationship between the historical specificity of the social formation and the programming practices of television contributes to our understanding of the ways in which popular cultural forms participate in the discourses of social life and diverge from the patterns of everyday experience.

NOTES

I wish to thank Beverly O'Neil for suggesting and participating in the survey of design journals and Robert Deming, Darryl Fox, and Lee Poague, who made helpful comments on earlier versions of this paper. Figure 1 is reprinted from *Industrial Design* 5, no. 2 (February 1958); Figure 2 is reprinted from *Industrial Design* 4, No. 11 (November 1957); Figures 3 and 4 are reprinted from *Industrial Design* 5, No. 1 (January 1958). All by permission of Design Publications, Inc. ©1957 and 1958. Figure 5 appears courtesy of Columbia Pictures.

   An earlier version of this paper, entitled "Suburban Family Sitcoms and Consumer Product Design: Addressing the Social Subjectivity of Homemakers in the 1950s," was presented to the 1986 International Television Studies Conference and appears in *Television and Its Audience: International Research Perspectives*, ed. Phillip Drummond and Richard Paterson (London: British Film Institute, 1988), pp. 38–60.

   1. In *Women: The Longest Revolution* (London: Virago, 1984), p. 18, Juliet Mitchell argues that women are bound up in this contradiction: "[Women] are fundamental to the human condition, yet in their economic, social and political roles, they are marginal. It is precisely this combination—fundamental and marginal at one and the same time—that has been fatal to them."

   2. Stuart Ewen and Elizabeth Ewen, *Channels of Desire: Mass Images and the Shaping of American Consciousness* (New York: McGraw-Hill, 1982), p. 235.

   3. Graham Murdock and Peter Golding, "Capitalism, Communication and Class Relations," and Stuart Hall, "Culture, Media and the 'Ideological Effect,'" in *Mass Communication and Society*, ed. James Curran, Michael Gurevitch, and Janet Woollacott (Beverly Hills: Sage, 1979), pp. 12, 36, 336–39.

   4. I began this study by considering prime-time network sitcoms with runs of three seasons or more from 1948 through 1960. Fourteen of these thirty-five sitcoms were structured around middle-class families living in suburban single-family dwellings. Eight of these fourteen defined the family unit as a breadwinner father, a homemaker mother, and children growing into adults: *The Ruggles* (1949–1952), *The Aldrich Family* (1949–1953), *The Stu Erwin Show* (1950–1955), *The Adventures of Ozzie and Harriet* (1952–1966), *Father Knows Best* (1954–1963), *Leave It to Beaver* (1957–1963), *The Donna Reed Show* (1958–1966), and *Dennis the Menace* (1959–1963).

      The other six suburban family sitcoms shared some of these traits, but centered their narratives on situations or characters other than the family ensemble: *Beulah* (1950–1953) focused on a black maid to an apparently broadly caricatured white middle-class family; *December Bride* (1954–1961) concerned an attractive, dating widow living with her daughter's family; *The Bob Cummings Show* (1955–1959) concentrated on the adventures of a playboy photographer living with his widowed sister and nephew in a suburban home; *I Married Joan* (1952–1955) focused on the zany adventures of the wife of a domestic court judge; *My Favorite Husband* (1953–1957) had a couple working for social status in the suburbs; and *Bachelor Father* (1957–1962) cared for his young niece in Beverly Hills.

This information was derived from the following sources: Tim Brooks and Earle Marsh, *The Complete Directory of Prime Time Network Television Shows, 1946–Present* (New York: Ballantine Books, 1981); Les Brown, *The New York Times Encyclopedia of Television* (New York: Times Books, 1977); Henry Castleman and Walter J. Podrazik, *The TV Schedule Book* (New York: McGraw-Hill, 1984).

5. Kenneth Rhodes, "Father of *Two* Families," *Cosmopolitan* (April 1956), p. 125.
6. Rhodes, "Father of *Two* Families," p. 125.; Bob Eddy, "Private Life of a Perfect Papa," *Saturday Evening Post* (27 April 1957), p. 29; Brooks and Marsh, *Complete Directory*, pp. 245–246.
7. Rhodes, "Father of *Two* Families," p. 125; Eddy, "Private Life," p. 29.
8. Newspaper critic John Crosby, quoted in Eddy, "Private Life," p. 29.
9. "TV's Eager Beaver," *Look* (27 May 1958), p. 68.
10. Brooks and Marsh, *Complete Directory*, pp. 340–41, 352–53.
11. Eddy, "Private Life," p. 29; Rhodes, "Father of *Two* Families," p. 126.
12. Eddy, "Private Life," p. 29; Rhodes, "Father of *Two* Families," p. 127.
13. "Jane Wyatt's Triple Threat," *Good Housekeeping* (October 1959), p. 48.
14. Eddy, "Private Life," p. 176; Dolores Hayden, *Redesigning the American Dream: The Future of Housing, Work and Family Life* (New York: Norton, 1984), p. 17.
15. Hayden, *Redesigning the American Dream*, p. 40; see also Gwendolyn Wright, *Building the Dream: A Social History of Housing in America* (Cambridge: MIT Press, 1981).
16. Hayden, *Redesigning the American Dream*, pp. 35, 38, 55; Wright, *Building the Dream*, pp. 246, 248.
17. Hayden, *Redesigning the American Dream* pp. 41–42; Wright, *Building the Dream*, p. 247.
18. Wright, *Building the Dream*, pp. 247–48.
19. Wright, *Building the Dream*, p. 248.
20. Hayden, *Redesigning the American Dream* pp. 55–56; Wright, *Building the Dream*, p. 256.
21. Hayden, *Redesigning the American Dream* pp. 63, 109.
22. Hayden, *Redesigning the American Dream* pp. 17–18; Wright, *Building the Dream*, pp. 254–55.
23. "The fifth international design conference at Aspen found 500 conferees at the crossroads, pondering the direction of the arts, and, every now and then, of the American consumer," *Industrial Design* 2, no. 4 (August 1955): 42; Avrom Fleishman, "M/R, a Survey of Problems, Techniques, Schools of Thought in Market Research: Part 1 of a Series," *Industrial Design* 5, no. 1 (January 1958): 26.
24. "Materialism, Leisure and Design," *Industrial Design* 4, no. 12 (December 1957): 33–34.
25. Dr. Wilson G. Scanlon, "Industrial Design and Emotional Immaturity," *Industrial Design* 4, no. 1 (January 1957): 68–69.
26. "Eleventh Annual ASID Conference: Three Days of Concentrated Design Discussion in Washington, D.C.," *Industrial Design* 2, no. 6 (December 1955): 123; Theodore Peterson, *Magazines in the Twentieth Century* (Urbana: University of Illinois Press, 1964), pp. 255, 298, 301–2.
27. "Eleventh Annual ASID Conference," p. 123.
28. Richard Tyler George, "The Process of Product Planning," *Industrial Design* 3, no. 5 (October 1956): 97–100. See also Deborah Allen, Avrom Fleishman, and Jane Fiske Mitarachi, "Report on Product Planning," *Industrial Design* 4, no. 6 (June 1957): 37–81; "Lawrence Wilson," *Industrial Design* 2, no. 5 (October 1955): 82–83; "Sundberg-Ferar," *Industrial Design* 2, no. 5 (October 1955): 86–87; "10 Work Elements of Product Planning," *Industrial Design* 4, no. 6 (June 1957): 47.
29. Avrom Fleishman, "M/R: Part 2," *Industrial Design* 5, no. 2 (February 1958): 42.
30. "IDI Discusses TV, Styling and Creativity," *Industrial Design* 4, no. 5 (May 1957): 67–68.
31. A. C. Neilsen Company, "The Neilsen Ratings in Perspective" (1980), p. 20; "IDI Discusses TV," pp. 67–68.
32. "IDI Discusses TV," pp. 67–68. On television technology and set design, see "Design Review," *Industrial Design* 6, no. 9 (August 1959): 89; "TV Sets Get Smaller and Smaller," *Industrial Design* 4, no. 1 (January 1957): 39–43; "Redesign: Philco Crops the Neck of the Picturetube to Be First with Separate-Screen Television," *Industrial Design* 5, no. 6 (June 1958): 52; "Design Review," *Industrial*

Design 6, no. 9 (August 1959): 88; Tenite advertisement, *Industrial Design* 6, no. 7 (July 1959): 23; Tenite advertisement, *Industrial Design* 8, no. 11 (November 1961): 25.

33. "The Consumer at IDI," *Industrial Design* 4, no. 11 (November 1957): 68–72.

34. Hayden, *Redesigning the American Dream*, p. 50

35. Fleishman, "M/R, a Survey of Problems," pp. 27, 29. While Fleishman recognized Paul Lazarsfeld's contribution to market research, this article did not mention Lazarsfeld's work in the television industry or his development of The Analyzer, an early instrument for audience measurement, for CBS. See Laurence Bergreen, *Look Now, Pay Later* (New York: New American Library, 1981), pp. 170–1.

36. Fleishman, "M/R, a Survey of Problems," p. 27.

37. Fleishman, "M/R, a Survey of Problems," p. 35.

38. Fleishman, "M/R, a Survey of Problems," p. 37.

39. Fleishman, "M/R, a Survey of Problems," p. 40.

40. Fleishman, "M/R, a Survey of Problems," pp. 41–42.

41. Fleishman, "M/R: Part 2," pp. 34–35; C. Wright Mills, "The Man in the Middle," *Industrial Design* 5, no. 11 (November 1958): 70; Don Wallace, "Report from Aspen," *Industrial Design* 5, no. 8 (August 1958): 85.

42. Mills, "The Man in the Middle," pp. 72–74.

43. "Jane Wyatt's Triple Threat," p. 48.

44. Danny Peary, "Remembering 'Father Knows Best'," in *TV Book*, ed. Judy Fireman (New York: Workman, 1977), pp. 173–75.

45. Long-running suburban family sitcoms which ran on network prime time during the early years of the women's movement were *Father Knows Best* (1954–1963), *Leave It to Beaver* (1957–1963), *The Donna Reed Show (1958–1966), The Dick Van Dyke Show (1961–1966)*, *Hazel* (1961–1966), *Dennis the Menace* (1959–1963), and *The Adventures of Ozzie and Harriet* (1952–1966). This information was obtained from Brooks and Marsh, *Complete Directory*, pp. 15–16, 193, 199–200, 211, 245–46, 322, 423 24.

Quar. Rev. of Film & Video, Vol. 11, pp. 85–105
Reprints available directly from the publisher
Photocopying permitted by license only

Harwood Academic Publishers, 1989
Printed in the United States of America

Women and Consumer Culture: A Selective Bibliography

Lynn Spigel and Denise Mann

This bibliography is meant to open up areas of research into the history of women and consumer culture. Since the industrial revolution and the increasing division of private and public spheres, women have been constituted as the caretakers of the home while their role as wage earners has been systematically undermined. This division has served a dual function—both ideological and economic. Not only have women been assigned the role of moral guardian of family life, but they also have been figured as the primary consumer of commodities for the household.

A wide range of media including advertising, film, broadcasting, and book publishing have historically idealized representations of the housewife/mother and have used this imagery to promote practices and institutions linked to consumerism. For example, a perfect crystallization of this came with the radio soap opera in the 1930s which linked a narrative organized around family melodrama to an array of advertised household products. Even while the "culture industries" have continually mobilized female desire for commodity goods and have constructed notions of femininity which are complicit with consumption, these industries have had to contend with resistance at the level of reception. As feminist analyses have shown, women might have read these idealized images subversively or at least "negotiated" the assumptions underlying these media forms. Furthermore, social histories of women suggest that the activities which comprise women's everyday lives form a locus of struggle with these dominant representations. These histories remind us that working-class women, subcultural groups, and even women of middle and upper-class status have not received these consumer dreams uncritically.

Here we bring together critical literature taken from what have traditionally been disparate academic fields and interests in order to facilitate research into areas relatively unexplored by film studies. We have selected books and articles on consumer culture and commodity display, magazines, mass-produced fiction aimed at women, and the social history of women in the age of industrialization. These references do not account for a comprehensive exploration of each field; instead, we have highlighted what we feel to be some of the most important work in each area, including standard texts and lesser known, but equally significant, studies.

LYNN SPIGEL is an assistant professor of Communication Arts at the University of Wisconsin-Madison, and author of the forthcoming book, Installing the Television Set.
DENISE MANN is writing her doctoral dissertation at UCLA on the star/product relation in early television programming and is an associate editor of Camera Obscura.

Consumer Culture and Commodity Display

This section takes as its starting point the emergence of commodity culture in the 1800s and its increasing penetration coincident with the growth of the advertising institution in the early 1900s. It focuses on the ways in which the commodity form has inserted itself into everyday life. We have included literature on fairs, shopping, department stores, supermarkets, fashion and beauty ideals, advertising history and theory, commodity theory, product design, wartime propaganda advertising, entertainment industries, and acculturation, as well as various forms of subcultural resistance to commodity culture.

Adburgham, Alison. *Shops and Shopping 1800–1914: Where, and in What Manner the Well-Dressed Englishwoman Bought Her Clothes.* Boston: Allen and Unwin, 1981.

Allen, Jeanne. "The Film Viewer as Consumer." *Quarterly Review of Film Studies* 5:4 (Fall 1980), pp. 481–501.

Allen, Robert C. "Motion Picture Exhibition in Manhattan, 1906–1912: Beyond the Nickelodeon." In *The American Movie Industry: The Business of Motion Pictures.* Ed. Gorham Kindem. Carbondale and Edwardsville: Southern Illinois University Press, 1982, pp. 12–24.

———. *Vaudeville and Film 1895–1915. A Study in Media Interaction.* New York: Arno Press, 1980.

Andrén, Gunnar, et al. *Rhetoric and Ideology in Advertising.* Stockholm: Liber, 1978.

Arlen, Michael J. *Thirty Seconds.* New York: Farrar, Straus and Giroux, 1980.

Atwan, Robert, Donald McQuade, and John W. Wright. *Edsels, Luckies, and Frigidaires: Advertising the American Way.* New York: Dell Publishing Co, 1979.

Baley, Stephen, ed. *In Good Shape: Style in Industrial Products, 1900–1960.* New York: Van Nostrand Reinhold, 1979.

Banner, Lois W. *American Beauty.* Chicago and London: University of Chicago Press, 1983.

Baran, Paul A., and Paul M. Sweezy. "The Absorption of Surplus: The Sales Effort." In *Monopoly Capital: An Essay on the American Economic and Social Order.* New York: Monthly Review Press, 1966, pp. 112–141.

Barnouw, Eric. *The Sponsor: Notes on a Modern Potentate.* Oxford: Oxford University Press, 1978.

Barthes, Roland. *The Fashion System.* Trans. Matthew Ward and Richard Howard. New York: Hill and Wang, 1983.

Batterberry, Michael, and Ariane Batterberry. *Mirror, Mirror: A Social History of Fashion.* New York: Holt, Rinehart and Winston, 1977.

Baudrillard, Jean. *For a Critique of the Political Economy of the Sign.* Trans. Charles Levin. St. Louis: Telos Press, 1981.

Benjamin, Walter. "The Work of Art in the Age of Mechanical Reproduction." In *Illuminations.* Reprinted from the French, 1936, Ed. Hannah Arendt. New York: Schocken, 1969, pp. 217–252.

Benson, Susan Porter. "Palaces of Consumption and Machines for Selling: The American Department Store, 1880–1940." *Radical History Review* 21 (Fall 1979), pp. 199–221.

Boorstin, Daniel. *The Americans: The Democractic Experience*. New York: Random House, 1973.

Bowlby, Rachel. *Just Looking: Consumer Culture in Dreiser, Gissing and Zola*. New York and London: Methuen, 1985.

Braverman, Harry. *Labor and Monopoly Capital: The Degradation of Work in the Twentieth Century*. New York: Monthly Review Press, 1974.

Bridges, Amy. "The Other Side of the Paycheck: Monopoly Capital and the Structure of Consumption." In *Capitalist Patriarchy and the Case for Socialist Feminism*. Ed. Zillah R. Eisenstein. New York: Monthly Review Press, 1979, pp. 190–205.

Browne, Ray B., and Marshall Fishwick, eds. *Icons of America*. Bowling Green, Ohio: Bowling Green University Popular Press, 1978.

Buck-Morss, Susan. "Benjamin's *Passagen-Werk:* Redeeming Mass Culture for the Revolution," *New German Critique* 29 (Spring-Summer 1983), pp. 211–240.

Burenstam, Linda Staffan. *The Harried Leisure Class*. New York: Columbia University Press, 1970.

Bush, Donald J. *The Streamline Decade*. New York: George Braziller, 1975.

Buxton, David. "Rock Music, the Star System and the Rise of Consumerism." *Telos* 57 (Fall 1983), pp. 93–106.

Carter, Erica. "Alice in the Consumer Wonderland: West German Case Studies in Gender and Consumer Culture." In *Gender and Generation*. Ed. Angela McRobbie and Mica Nava. London: Macmillan, 1984, pp. 185–214.

Chaney, David. "The Department Store as a Cultural Form." *Theory, Culture, and Society* 1:3 (1983), pp. 22–43.

Chibnall, Stephen. "Whistle and Zoot: The Changing Meaning of a Suit of Clothes." *History Workshop Journal* 20 (Autumn 1985), pp. 56–81.

Clarke, John, Stuart Hall, Tony Jefferson, and Brian Roberts. "Subcultures, Cultures and Class." *Working Papers in Cultural Studies* 7-8 (Summer 1975), pp. 8–79.

Cosgrove, Stuart. "The Zoot-Suit and Style Warfare." *History Workshop Journal* 18 (Autumn 1984), pp. 77–91.

Davis, Dorothy. *Fairs, Shops, and Supermarkets: A History of English Shopping*. Toronto: University of Toronto Press, 1966.

Debord, Guy. *Society of the Spectacle*. Detroit: Black and Red, 1977.

de Certeau, Michel. "On the Oppositional Practices of Everyday Life." *Social Text* 3 (1980), pp. 3–43.

Douglas, Mary Tew, and Baron Isherwood. *The World of Goods*. New York: Basic Books, 1979.

Eckert, Charles. "The Carole Lombard in Macy's Window." *Quarterly Review of Film Studies* 3:1 (Winter 1978), pp. 1–21.

Erenberg, Lewis. *Steppin' Out: New York Nightlife and the Transformation of American Culture, 1890–1930*. Chicago: University of Chicago Press, 1981.

Ewen, Elizabeth. *Immigrant Women in the Land of Dollars: Life and Culture on the Lower East Side, 1890–1925*. New York: Monthly Review Press, 1985.

———. "City Lights: Immigrant Women and the Rise of the Movies." *Signs* 5:3, Supplement (Spring 1980), pp. S45–S66.

Ewen, Stuart. "Advertising as Social Production." *Radical America* 3 (May 1969), pp. 42–56.

————. *Captains of Consciousness: Advertising and the Social Roots of the Consumer Culture.* New York: McGraw-Hill, 1976.

Ewen Stuart, and Elizabeth Ewen. "Americanization and Consumption." *Telos* 37 (Fall 1978), pp. 5–21.

————. *Channels of Desire: Mass Images and the Shaping of American Consciousness.* New York: McGraw-Hill, 1982.

Featherstone, Mike. "The Body in Consumer Culture." *Theory, Culture and Society* 1:2 (Autumn 1982), pp. 18–33.

————. "Consumer Culture: An Introduction." *Theory, Culture and Society* 1:3 (1983), pp. 4–9.

Ferry, John William. *A History of the Department Store.* New York: Macmillan, 1960.

Forty, Adrian. *Objects of Desire: Design and Society From Wedgewood to IBM* New York: Pantheon Books, 1986.

Fox, Frank W. *Madison Avenue Goes to War: The Strange Military Career of American Advertising, 1941–1945.* Provo, UT: Brigham Young University Press, 1975.

Fox, Richard Wightman, and T.J. Jackson Lears, eds. *The Culture of Consumption: Critical Essays in American History, 1880–1980.* New York: Pantheon Books, 1983.

Fox, Steven. *The Mirror Makers: A History of American Advertising and Its Creators.* New York: Morrow, 1984.

Fox-Genovese, Elizabeth. "Yves Saint Laurent's Peasant Revolution." *Marxist Perspectives* 1:2 (Summer 1978), pp. 58–93.

Frederick, Christine McGoffey. *Selling Mrs. Consumer.* New York: The Business Course, 1929.

Gabler, William G. "The Evolution of American Advertising in the Nineteenth Century." *Journal of Popular Culture* 11:4 (Spring 1978), pp. 763–771.

Gaines, Jane. "The Popular Icon as Commodity and Sign: The Circulation of Betty Grable, 1941–55." Diss. Northwestern University, 1982.

Gaines, Jane, and Charlotte Herzog. "The Comedy of Inequality: Hildy Johnson and the Man-Tailored Suit." *Film Reader* 5 (Winter 1982), pp. 232–246.

————. "Puffed Sleeves Before Teatime: Joan Crawford, Adrian and Women Audiences." *Wide Angle* 6:4 (1985), pp. 24–33.

Giedion, Siegfried. *Mechanization Takes Command: A Contribution to Anonymous History.* New York and London: W.W. Norton, 1948.

Ginsburg, Madeleine. "Rags to Riches: Second-Hand Clothes Trade, 1700–1978." *Costume, The Journal of the Costume Society* 14 (1980), pp. 121–135.

Goffman, Erving. *Gender Advertisements.* New York: Harper and Row, 1981.

Goldman, Robert L. "The Meanings of Leisure in Corporate America, 1890–1930." Diss. Duke University, 1977.

Gordon, Eleanor, and Jean Nerenberg. "Everywomen's Jewelry: Early Plastics and Equality in Fashion." *Journal of Popular Culture* 13:4 (Spring 1980), pp. 629–644.

Griff, Mason. "Advertising—The Central Institution of Mass Society." *Diogenes* 68 (Winter 1969), pp. 120–137.

Gurevitch, Michael, Tony Bennett, James Curran, and Janet Woollacott, eds. *Culture, Society and the Media.* London and New York: Methuen, 1982.

Gustafson, Robert. "The Power of the Screen: The Influence of Edith Head's Film Designs on the Retail Fashion Market." *The Velvet Light Trap* 19 (1982) pp. 8–15.

Hall, Stuart. "Culture, the Media and the 'Ideological Effect'." In *Mass Communications and Society*. Ed. James Curran et al. London: Arnold, 1977, pp. 315–348.

Hall, Stuart, and Dorothy Hobson, Andrew Lowe, and Paul Willis, eds. *Culture, Media, Language*. London: Hutchinson, 1980

Haralovich, Mary Beth. "Movie Advertising: Industrial and Social Forces and Effects, 1930–1948." Diss. University of Wisconsin, Madison, 1984.

Harris, Neil. "The Drama of Consumer Desire." In *Yankee Enterprise: The Rise of the American System of Manufactures*. Washington, D.C.: Smithsonian Institution Press, 1981, pp. 189–216.

Haug, Wolfgang Fritz. *Critique of Commodity Aesthetics: Appearance, Sexuality, and Advertising in Capitalist Society*. Trans. Robert Bock. Cambridge: Polity Press, 1986.

Hebdige, Dick. *Subcultures: The Meaning of Style*. London: Methuen, 1979.

Hendrickson, Robert. *The Grand Emporiums: The Illustrated History of America's Great Department Stores*. New York: Stein and Day, 1979.

Higashi, Sumiko. "Cinderella vs. Statistics: The Silent Movie Heroine as a Jazz-Age Working Girl." In *Woman's Being, Woman's Place: Female Identity and Vocation in American History*. Ed. Mary Kelly. Boston: G.K. Hall & Co., 1979, pp. 109–126.

————. *Virgins, Vamps, and Flappers: The American Silent Movie Heroine*. St. Albans, VT: Eden Press Women's Publications, 1978.

Horkheimer, Max, and T.W. Adorno. "The Culture Industry: Enlightenment as Mass Deception." In *Dialectic of Enlightenment*. Reprinted from the German, 1947. New York: Seabury Press, 1972, pp. 120–167.

Horowitz, R.T. "From Elite Fashion to Mass Fashion." *Archives Européenes de Sociologie* 16 (1975), pp. 283–295.

Jameson, Fredric. "Postmodernism and Consumer Society." In *The Anti-Aesthetic: Essays in Postmodern Culture*. Ed. Hal Foster. Port Townsend, WA: Big Press, 1983, pp. 111–125.

Jewell, Richard B. "Hollywood and Radio: Competition and Partnership in the 1930s" *Historical Journal of Film, Radio and Television* 4:2 (1984), pp. 125–141.

Jhally, Sut, Stephen Kline, and William Leiss. "Magic in the Marketplace: An Empirical Test for Commodity Fetishism." *Canadian Journal of Political and Social Theory* 9:3 (Fall 1985), pp. 1–22.

Kando, Thomas M. *Leisure and Popular Culture in Transition*. St. Louis: Mosby, 1980.

Kasson, John F. *Amusing the Millions: Coney Island at the Turn of the Century*. New York: Hill and Wang, 1978.

Kellner, Douglas. "Critical Theory, Commodities and the Consumer Society." *Theory, Culture and Society* 1:3 (1983), pp. 66–81.

Kidwell, Claudia B., and Margaret C. Christman. *Suiting Everyone: The Democratization of Clothing in America*. Washington, D.C.: Smithsonian Institution Press, 1974.

Kline, Stephen, and William Leiss. "Advertising, Needs and Commodity Fetishism." *Canadian Journal of Political and Social Theory* 2:1 (1978), pp. 5–30.

Kowinski, William Severini. *The Malling of America: An Inside Look at the Great Consumer Paradise*. New York: Morrow, 1985.

Kracauer, Siegfried. "The Mass Ornament." *New German Critique* 5 (Spring 1975), pp. 67–76.

Lakoff, Robin Tolmach, and Raquel L. Scherr. *Face Value: The Politics of Beauty.* London and Boston: Routledge and Kegan Paul, 1984.

La Place, Maria. "Bette Davis and the Ideal of Consumption: A Look at *Now Voyager.*" *Wide Angle* 6:4 (1985), pp. 34–43.

Leach, William R. "Transformations in a Culture of Consumption: Women and Department Stores, 1890–1925." *Journal of American History* 71 (1984), pp. 317–342.

Lears, T.J. Jackson. *No Place of Grace: Antimodernism and the Transformation of American Culture, 1880–1920.* New York: Pantheon Books, 1981.

———. "Some Versions of Fantasy: Toward a Cultural History of American Advertising, 1880–1930." *Prospects* 9 (1984), pp. 349–405.

Lefebvre, Henri. *Everyday Life in the Modern World.* Trans. Sacha Rabinovitch. New York: Harper Torchbooks, 1971.

Leiss, William. "The Icons of the Marketplace." *Theory, Culture and Society* 1:3 (1983), pp. 10–21.

———. *The Limits to Satisfaction: An Essay on the Problem of Needs and Commodities.* Toronto: University of Toronto Press, 1976.

———. "Needs, Exchange and the Fetishization of Objects." *Canadian Journal of Political and Social Theory* 2 (1978), pp. 29–48.

Levy, Sidney J. "Interpreting Consumer Mythology: A Structural Approach to Consumer Behavior." *Journal of Marketing* 45:3 (Summer 1981), pp. 49–61.

Ley, Sandra. *Fashion for Everyone: The Story of Ready-to-Wear, 1870–1970.* New York: Charles Scribner's Sons, 1975.

Leymore, Varda Langholz. *Hidden Myth: Structure and Symbolism in Advertising.* London: Heinemann Educational, 1975.

Lynd, Robert S. "The People as Consumers." In *Recent Social Trends in the United States Volume II.* President's Research Committee on Social Trends. New York and London: McGraw-Hill, 1933, pp. 857–911.

Lynd, Robert S., and Helen Merrell Lynd. *Middletown: A Study in Contemporary American Culture.* New York: Harcourt Brace, 1929.

———. *Middletown in Transition: A Study in Cultural Conflicts.* New York: Harcourt Brace, 1937.

MacDonald, J. Fred. "Government Propaganda in Commercial Radio—The Case of Treasury Star Parade, 1942–1943." *Journal of Popular Culture* 12:2 (Fall 1979), pp. 285–304.

Marchland, Roland. *Advertising the American Dream: Making Way for Modernity, 1920–1940.* Berkeley: University of California Press, 1985.

May, Lary. *Screening Out the Past: The Birth of Mass Culture and the Motion Picture Industry.* Chicago and London: University of Chicago Press, 1980.

Mayne, Judith. "Immigrants and Spectators." *Wide Angle* 5:2 (1983), pp. 32–41.

McCannell, D. *The Tourist: A New Theory of the Leisure Class.* London: Macmillan, 1976.

McKendrick, Neil. "The Commercialization of Fashion." In *The Birth of a Consumer Society: The Commercialization of Eighteenth-Century England.* Ed. Neil McKendrick et al. Bloomington: Indiana University Press, 1982, pp. 34–99.

———. "The Consumer Revolution of Eighteenth-Century England." In *The Birth of a Consumer Society: The Commercialization of Eighteenth-Century England.* Ed. Neil McKendrick et al. Bloomington: Indiana University Press, 1982, pp. 1–33.

McQuaid, Kim. "An American Owenite: Edward A. Filene and the Parameters of Industrial Reform, 1890–1937." *American Journal of Economics and Sociology* 35:1 (January 1976), pp. 77–94.

McRobbie, Angela. "Jackie: The Ideology of Adolescent Femininity." In *Popular Culture: Past and Present* Ed. Bernard Waites et al. London: Croom Helm and The Open University Press, 1982, pp. 263–283.

———. "Settling Accounts with Subcultures: A Feminist Critique." *Screen Education* 34 (1980), pp. 37–49.

McRobbie, Angela, and Jenny Garber. "Girls and Subcultures: An Exploration." Working Papers in Cultural Studies Special-Issue, *Resistance Through Rituals*, 7-8 (Summer 1975), pp. 209–222.

Meikle, Jeffrey L. *Twentieth Century Limited: Industrial Design in America, 1925–1939.* Philadelphia: Temple University Press, 1979.

Merritt, Russell. "Nickelodeon Theaters 1905–1914: Building an Audience for the Movies." In *The American Film Industry.* Ed. Tino Balio. Madison: University of Wisconsin Press, 1976.

Miller, Michael Barry. *The Bon Marché: Bourgeois Culture and the Department Store, 1869–1920.* Princeton: Princeton University Press, 1981.

Mowry, George E. *The Twenties: Fords, Flappers and Fanatics.* Englewood Cliffs: Prentice-Hall, 1963.

Mukerji, Chandra. *From Graven Images: Patterns of Modern Materialism.* New York: Columbia University Press, 1983.

Patterson, James M. "Marketing and the Working-Class Family." In *Blue Collar World.* Ed. Arthur B. Shostak and William Goldberg. New York: Prentice-Hall, 1964.

Perutz, Kathrin. *Beyond the Looking Glass: America's Beauty Culture.* New York: Morrow, 1970.

Pevsner, Nikolaus. *Pioneers of Modern Design: From William Morris to Walter Gropius.* Harmondsworth and Middlesex, Penguin Books, 1975.

Polhemus, Ted, and L. Procter. *Fashion and Anti-Fashion: An Anthropology of Clothing and Adornment.* London: Cox and Wyman, 1978.

Pollay, Richard W. "The Importance, and the Problems, of Writing the History of Advertising." *Journal of Advertising History* 1 (1977), pp. 3–5.

———. "The Subsiding Sizzle: A Descriptive History of Print Advertising, 1900–1980," *Journal of Marketing* 3 (Summer 1985), pp. 24–37.

Pope, Daniel. *The Making of Modern Advertising.* New York: Basic Books, 1983.

Pulos, Arthur J. *American Design Ethic: A History of Industrial Design.* Cambridge: MIT Press, 1983.

Radar, Edmond. "The Manifestations of Fashion as a Phenomenon of Social Psychology." *Diogenes* 68 (Winter 1969), pp. 80–97.

Rapping, Elayne. "Tupperware and Women." *Radical America* 14:6 (November-December 1980), pp. 39–48.

Roach, Mary Ellen, and Joanne Bubolz Eicher, eds. *Dress, Adornment and the Social Order.* New York: John Wiley & Sons, 1965.

Ryan, Mary P. "The Projection of a New Womanhood: The Movie Moderns in the 1920s." In *Our American Sisters: Women in American Life and Thought.* Ed. Jean E.

Friedman and William G. Shade. 2nd ed. Boston: Allyn and Bacon, 1976, pp. 366–384.

Rydell, Robert W. *All the World's Fair: Vision of Empire at American International Expositions, 1876–1916*. Chicago: University of Chicago Press, 1985.

Schudson, Michael. *Advertising, the Uneasy Persuasion: Its Dubious Impact on American Society*. New York: Basic Books, 1984.

———. "Criticizing the Critics of Advertising: Towards a Sociological View of Marketing." *Media, Culture and Society* 3 (January 1981), pp. 3–12.

Schultze, Quentin James. "Advertising, Science, and Professionalism, 1885–1917." Diss. University of Illinois, Urbana-Champaign, 1978.

Silva, Rafael Drinot. "Advertising: The Production and Consumption of Daily Life." In *Communication and Class Struggle, An Anthology Volume I*. Ed. Armand Mattelart and Seth Sieglaub. New York: International General, 1979, pp. 353–358.

Slotkin, Richard. *The Fatal Environment: The Myth of the Frontier in the Age of Industrialization, 1800–1890*. New York: Atheneum, 1985.

Spalding, John W. "1928: Radio Becomes a Mass Advertising Medium." *Journal of Broadcasting* 8 (1963–64), pp. 31–44.

Sparke, Penny. *An Introduction to Design and Culture in the Twentieth Century*. London: Allen & Unwin, 1986.

Springman, Jay K., and Carol Pratt. "The Home That Radio Built." *Journal of Popular Culture* 12:2 (Fall 1979), pp. 265–274.

Sproles, George B. "Analyzing Fashion Life Cycles: Principles and Perspectives." *Journal of Marketing* 45:4 (1981), pp. 116–124.

Susman, Warren I. *Culture as History: The Transformation of American Society in the Twentieth Century*. New York: Pantheon Books, 1984.

Turim, Maureen. "Designing Women: The Emergence of the New Sweetheart Line." *Wide Angle* 6:2 (1984), pp. 4–11.

———. "Fashion Shapes: Film, the Fashion Industry and the Image of Women." *Socialist Review* 71:13:5 (September-October 1983), pp. 79–96.

———. "Gentleman Consume Blondes." *Wide Angle* 1:1 (1976), pp. 68–77; (1979), pp. 52–59; rpt. in *Movies and Methods II*. Ed. Bill Nichols. Berkeley: University of California Press, 1985, pp. 369–378.

Vries, Leonard, and James Laver. *Victorian Advertisements*. London: John Murray, 1968.

Waldman, Diane. "From Midnight Shows to Marriage Vows: Woman, Exploitation, and Exhibition." *Wide Angle* 6:2 (1984), pp. 40–48.

Weimann, Jeanne Madeline. *The Fair Women*. Chicago: Academy, 1981.

Williams, Raymond. "Advertising: The Magic System." In *Problems in Materialism and Culture*. London: Verso, 1980, pp. 170–195.

Williams, Rosalind H. *Dream Worlds: Mass Consumption in Late Nineteenth-Century France*. Berkeley: University of California Press, 1982.

Williamson, Elizabeth. "Advertising." In *Handbook of American Popular Culture Volume 2*. Ed. M. Thomas Inge. Westport, Conn., Greenwood Press, 1980.

Williamson, Judith. *Decoding Advertisements: Ideology and Meaning in Advertising*. New York: Marion Boyars, 1979.

Willis, Ellen. "Consumerism and Women." *Socialist Revolution* 3 (May-June 1970), pp. 76–82.

Willis, Susan. "Should We Re-Cycle Marx?" *Praxis* 2 (Fall 1976), pp. 231–238.

Wilson, Elizabeth. *Adorned in Dreams: Fashion and Modernity.* London: Virago, 1985.

Wilson, G.B.L. "Domestic Appliances." In *A History of Technology Volume VII, Part 2.* Ed. T.I. Williams. Oxford: Clarendon Press, 1978.

Winship, Janice. "Handling Sex." *Media, Culture and Society* 3 (1981), pp. 6–18.

———. "Sexuality for Sale." In *Culture, Media, Language.* Ed. Stuart Hall, et al. London: Hutchinson, 1980, pp. 217–223.

Rereading Magazines

By the late 1800s women were the primary readership for popular magazines in America. Editorial content and advertising copy were devoted to the female reader. Recent literature has examined this privileged relationship between women and magazines, both historically and critically. Some of these references use magazines as indices of larger cultural issues, others analyze the rhetorical and discursive strategies employed, and still others focus on relationships among magazines and the film, radio, and television industries.

Adburgham, Alison. *Women in Print: Writing Women and Women's Magazines from the Restoration to the Accession of Victoria.* London: Allen and Unwin, 1972.

Alderson, C. *Magazines Teenagers Read.* Oxford: Pergamon, 1968.

Blum, Stella, ed. *Everyday Fashions of the Twenties as Pictured in Sears and Other Catalogues.* New York: Dover Publications, 1981.

———. *Victorian Fashion and Costumes from Harper's Bazaar: 1867–1898.* New York: Dover, 1974.

Brown, Bruce W. "Family Intimacy in Magazine Advertising: 1920–1977." *Journal of Communication* 32:3 (Summer 1982), pp. 173–183.

Butler-Flora, Cornelia. "The Passive Female: Her Comparative Image by Class and Culture in Women's Magazine Fiction." *Journal of Marriage and the Family* 33 (August 1971), pp. 434–444.

Cardinale, Susan. *Special Issues of Serials About Women, 1965–1975.* Monticello, IL: Council of Planning Librarians. 1976.

Cohn, David. *The Good Old Days: A History of American Morals and Manners as Seen Through the Sears, Roebuck Catalogs, 1905 to the Present.* New York: Simon and Schuster, 1940.

Compaine, Benjamin M. "The Magazine Industry: Developing the Special Interest Audience." *Journal of Communication* 30:2 (Spring 1980), pp. 98–103.

Dancyger, Irene. *A World of Women: An Illustrated History of Women's Magazines.* Dublin: Gilland MacMillan, 1978.

Daniel, Walter C. "Langston Hughes' Introduction to *Esquire* Magazine." *Journal of Popular Culture* 12:4 (Spring 1979), pp. 620–623.

Dewin, Polly. *Vogue Book of Fashion Photography 1919–1979.* New York: Simon and Schuster, 1979.

Dorfman, Ariel. "Salvation and Wisdom of the Common Man: The Theology of the *Reader's Digest.* *Praxis* 1:3 (1976), pp. 41–56.

Earnshaw, Stella. "Advertising and the Media: The Case of Women's Magazines." *Media, Culture and Society* 6 (1984), pp. 411–421.

Edger, Neal L. *A History and Bibliography of American Magazines 1810–1820*. Metuchen, NJ: Scarecrow Press, 1975.

Elwin, Malcolm. *Victorian Wallflowers: A Panoramic Survey of the Popular Literary Periodicals*. Port Washington, NY: Kennikat Press, 1966.

Entrikin, Isabelle Webb. *Sarah Josepha Hale and Godey's Lady's Book*. Lancaster, PA: Lancaster Press, 1946.

Ferguson, Marjorie. "Imagery and Ideology: The Cover Photographs of Traditional Women's Magazines." In *Hearth and Home: Images of Women in the Mass Media*. Ed. Gaye Tuchman, Arlene Kaplan Daniels, and James Benet. New York: Oxford University Press, 1978, pp. 97–115.

Finley, Ruth E. *The Lady of Godey's: Sarah Josepha Hale*. Philadelphia: J.B. Lippincott Co., 1931.

Ford, James L. *Magazines for Millions: The Story of Specialized Publications*. Carbondale: Southern Illinois University Press, 1969.

Friedan, Betty. *The Feminine Mystique*. New York: W.W. Norton & Co. 1963.

Gabor, Mark. *The Illustrated History of Girlie Magazines: From the National Police Gazette to the Present*. New York: Harmony Books, 1983.

Gaines, Jane. "War, Women, and Lipstick: Fan Magazines in the 1940's." *Heresies* 19 (January 1986).

Gerbner, George. "The Social Role of the Confession Magazine." *Social Problems* 6 (Summer 1958), pp. 29–40.

Goodstone, Tony. *The Pulps: Fifty Years of American Pop Culture*. New York: Chelsea House, 1970.

Greene, Theodore. *America's Heroes. The Changing Models of Success in American Magazines*. New York: Oxford University Press, 1970.

Hall, Carolyn. *The Thirties in Vogue*. New York: Harmony Books, 1985.

Hodgson, Pat. *The War Illustrators*. London: Osprey, 1977.

Hoekstra, Ellen. "The Pedestal Myth Reinforced: Women's Magazine Fiction, 1900–1920." In *New Dimensions in Popular Culture*. Ed. Russel B. Nye. Bowling Green, OH: Bowling Green University Popular Press, 1972, pp. 45–58.

Holder, Stephen C. "The Family Magazine and the American People." *Journal of Popular Culture* 7:2 (Fall 1973), pp. 264–279.

Honey, Maureen. "The 'Celebrity' Magazines." In *New Dimensions in Popular Culture*. Ed. Russel B. Nye. Bowling Green, OH: Bowling Green University Popular Press, 1972, pp. 59–77.

———. *Creating Rosie the Riveter: Class, Gender and Propaganda During WWII*. Amherst: University of Massachusetts Press, 1984.

———. "Images of Women in the *Saturday Evening Post*, 1931–1936." *Journal of Popular Culture* 10 (Fall 1976), pp. 352–58.

———. "Recruiting Women For War Work: OWI and the Magazine Industry During World War II." *Journal of American Culture* 3:1 (Spring 1980), pp. 47–52.

Jones, Robert Kenneth. *The Shudder Pulps: A History of the Weird Menace Magazines of the 1930's*. West Linn, OR: FAX Collector's Editions, 1975.

Kallan, Richard A., and Robert D. Brooks. "The Playmate of the Month: Naked But Nice." *Journal of Popular Culture* 8:2 (Fall 1974), pp. 328–336.

Kunzle, David. "*The Reader's Digest*—A Self-Image." *Praxis* 1:3 (1976), pp. 38–40.

Leman, Joy. "The Advice of a Real Friend: Codes of Intimacy and Oppression in Women's Magazines, 1937–1955." *Women's Studies International Quarterly* 3:1 (1980), pp. 63–78.

Lewis, Benjamin Morgan. *An Introduction to American Magazines, 1800–1810.* Ann Arbor: University of Michigan, Department of Library Science, 1961.

Martel, Martin, and George McCall. "Reality-Orientation and the Pleasure Principle: A Study of American Mass-Periodical Fiction (1890–1955)." In *People, Society and Mass Communications.* Ed. Lewis Dexter and David White. New York: Free Press, 1964, pp. 283–334.

Mattelart, Michele. "Notes on 'Modernity': A Way of Reading Women's Magazines." In *Communication and Class Struggle, An Anthology Volume I.* Ed. Armond Mattelart and Seth Sieglaub. New York: International General, 1979, pp. 158–170.

McCracken, Ellen. "Demystifying *Cosmopolitan*: Five Critical Methods." *Journal of Popular Culture* 16:2 (Fall 1982), pp. 30–42.

McCullum, Pamela. "World Without Conflict: Magazines for Working Women." *Canadian Forum* 55 (September 1975), pp. 42–44.

Millum, Trevor. *Images of Woman: Advertising in Women's Magazines.* Totawa, NJ: Rowan and Littlefield, 1975.

Moskowitz, Sam, ed. *Under the Moons of Mars: A History and Anthology of "the Scientific Romance" in the Munsey Magazines, 1912–1920.* New York: Holt, Rinehart and Winston, 1970.

Mott, Frank Luther. *A History of American Magazines, 1885–1905.* Cambridge: Harvard University Press, 1957.

Noel, Mary. *Villains Galore: The Heyday of the Popular Story Weekly.* New York: Macmillan, 1954.

Peterson, Theodore. *Magazines in the Twentieth Century.* Urbana: University of Illinois Press, 1964.

Phillips, E. Barbara. "Magazine Heroines: Is *Ms.* Just Another Member of the *Family Circle?*" In *Hearth and Home: Images of Women in the Mass Media* Ed. Gaye Tuchman, Arlene Kaplan Daniels, and James Benet. New York: Oxford University Press, 1978, pp. 116–129.

Probert, Christina. *Lingerie in Vogue Since 1910.* New York: Abbeville Press, 1981.

Ricciotti, Dominic. "Popular Art in *Godey's Lady's Book:* An Image of American Woman, 1830–1860." *History of New Hampshire* 27:1 (1972), pp. 3–26.

Richardson, Lyon Norman. *A History of Early American Magazines, 1741–1789.* New York: Octagon Books, 1966.

Rossi, Lee D. "The Whore vs. The Girl-Next-Door: Stereotypes of Woman in *Playboy, Penthouse,* and *Oui.*" *Journal of Popular Culture* 9:1 (Summer 1975), pp. 90-94.

Sampson, Robert. *Yesterday's Faces: A Study of Series Characters in the Early Pulp Magazines.* Bowling Green, OH: Bowling Green University Popular Press, 1983.

Shattock, Joanne, and Michael Wolff. *The Victorian Periodical Press, Samplings and Soundings.* Toronto: University of Toronto Press, 1982.

Social Research, Inc. Report. *The Differing Meanings of Women's Magazines and Television.* Chicago: 1954.

Sonenschein, David. "Love and Sex in the Romance Magazines." *Journal of Popular Culture* 4:2 (1970), pp. 398–409.

Stearns, Bertha-Monica. "Before *Godey's*." *American Literature* 2 (1930), pp. 248–255.

Stein, Sally A. "The Composite Photographic Image and the Composition of Consumer Ideology." *Art Journal* 41:1 (Spring 1981), pp. 39–45.

———. "The Graphic Ordering of Desire: Modernization of a Middle-Class Women's Magazine, 1914–1939." *Heresies* 19 (January 1986).

Stewart, Penni. "He Admits . . . but She Confesses." *Women's Studies International Quarterly* 3:1 (1980), pp. 105–114.

Stineman, Esther. "What the Ladies Were Reading: Popular Women's Magazines in America, 1875–1975." M.A. Thesis. University of Chicago, 1976.

Tassin, Algernon Vivier. *The Magazine in America*. New York: Dodd Mead Co. 1916.

Tebbel, John. *George Horace Lorimer and The Saturday Evening Post*. Garden City, NY: Doubleday, 1948.

Thompson, Eleanor Wolf. *Education for Ladies, 1830–1860*. New York: King's Crown Press, 1947.

Tortora, Phyllis. "Fashion Magazines Mirror Changing Role of Women." *Journal of Home Economics* 65:3 (March 1973), pp. 19–23.

Trahey, Jane, ed. *Harper's Bazaar: 100 Years of the American Female*. New York: Random House, 1967.

Watson, Melvin Ray. *Magazine Serials and the Essay Tradition, 1746–1820*. Baton Rouge: Louisiana State University Press, 1956.

White, Cynthia L. *Women's Magazines 1693–1968*. London: Michael Joseph, 1970.

Wilson, Christopher P. "The Rhetoric of Consumption: Mass-Market Magazines and the Demise of the Gentle Reader, 1880–1920." In *The Culture of Consumption: Critical Essays in American History, 1880–1980*. Ed. Richart Wightman Fox and T.J. Jackson Lears. New York: Pantheon Books, 1983, pp. 39–64.

Winick, Charles. "Teenagers, Satire, and *Mad*." In *People, Society and Mass Communications*. Ed. Lewis Dexter and David White. New York: Free Press, 1964.

Winship, Janice. " 'Options—for the Way You Want to Live Now', or a Magazine for Superwoman." *Theory, Culture and Society* 1:3 (1983), pp. 44–65.

Wood, James Playsted. *Magazines in the United States: Their Social and Economic Influences*. New York: Ronald Press, 1949.

Woodward, Helen. *The Lady Persuaders*. New York: Ivan Obolensky, 1960.

Zuilen, A.J. van. *The Life Cycle of Magazines: A Historical Study of the Decline and Fall of the General Mass Audience Magazine in the United States During the Period 1946–1972*. Vithoorn: Graduate Press, 1977.

Mass-Produced "Women's Fiction"

The publishing and broadcasting industries have historically appealed to a female public/consumer. In recent years feminist critics have explored the popularity of mass-produced fiction—including the woman's film, radio and television soap operas, prime-time serial dramas, as well as gothic and romance paperback novels. Why do women continue to consume these fictions? What satisfactions and pleasures do these texts offer? How do female readers interpret these narratives? How do the texts interact with the woman's everyday life? And what are the "ideological effects" and/or utopian values? In the articles and books referenced here, these questions are explored through a variety of approaches including textual analysis, narrative theory, reception theory, audience research, as well as institutional and historical analysis. We have isolated works which deal directly with "women's fiction"; however, it should be noted that many of these studies draw upon the literature on melodrama which is not included here.

Allen Robert C. "On Reading Soap Operas: A Semiotic Primer." In *Regarding Television.* Ed. E. Ann Kaplan. Los Angeles: University Publications of America, 1983, pp. 97–108.

———. "The Guilding Light: Soap Opera as Economic Product and Cultural Document." In *American History/American Television.* Ed. John E. O'Connor. New York: Frederick Ungar Publishing Co., 1983, pp. 306–327.

———. *Speaking of Soap Operas.* Chapel Hill and London: University of North Carolina Press, 1985.

Ang, Ien. *Watching Dallas: Soap Opera and the Melodramatic Imagination.* Trans. Della Couling. New York and London: Methuen, 1985.

Bathrick, Serafina Kent. "The True Woman and the Family Film: The Industrial Production of Memory." Diss. University of Wisconsin, Madison, 1981.

Baym, Nina. *Women's Fiction: A Guide to Novels by and about Women in America, 1800–1870.* Ithaca: Cornell University Press, 1978.

Beurkel-Rothfuss, Nancy L., and Sandra Mayes. "Soap Opera Viewing: The Cultivation Effect." *Journal of Communication* 31:3 (Summer 1981), pp. 108–115.

Bode, Carl. "The Scribbling Women: The Domestic Novel Rules the 'Fifties'." In *The Anatomy of American Popular Culture, 1840–1861.* Berkeley: University of California Press, 1959, pp. 169-187.

Brown, Herbert Ross. *The Sentimental Novel in America, 1789–1860.* Durham: Duke University Press, 1940.

Byars, Jackie. "Gender Representation in American Family Melodramas of the 1950s." Diss. University of Texas, Austin, 1983.

Cantor, Muriel, and Susanne Pingree. *The Soap Opera.* Beverly Hills, Sage, 1983.

Derry, Charles. "Television Soap Opera: Incest, Bigamy, and Fatal Disease." *Journal of the University Film and Video Association* 35:1 (Winter 1983), pp. 4–16.

Doane, Mary Ann. "*Caught* and *Rebecca*: The Inscription of Feminity as Absence." *Enclitic* 5:2/6:1 (Fall 1981-Spring 1982), pp. 75–89.

———. "The Clinical Eye: Medical Discourses in the 'Woman's Film' of the 1940's." *Poetics Today* 6:1/6:2 (1985), pp. 205–227.

Douglas, Ann. *The Feminization of American Culture.* New York: Knopf, 1977.

———. "Soft-Porn Culture." *New Republic* 30 (August 1980), pp. 25–29.

Dyer, Richard, ed. *Coronation Street.* London: British Film Institute, 1981.

Edmondson, Madeleine, and David Rounds. *The Soaps, Daytime Serials of Radio and Television.* New York: Stein and Day, 1973.

Feuer, Jane. "Melodrama, Serial Form and Television Today." *Screen* 25:1 (January-February 1984), pp. 4–16.

Flitterman, Sandy. "The Real Soap Operas: TV Commercials." In *Regarding Televi-*

sion. Ed. E. Ann Kaplan. Los Angeles: University Publications of America, 1983, pp. 84–96.

Franzwa, Helen H. "Working Women in Fact and Fiction." *Journal of Communication* 24:2 (Spring 1974), pp. 104–109.

Gilbert, Sandra M., and Susan Gubar. *The Madwoman in the Attic: The Woman Writer and the Nineteenth-Century Literary Imagination*. New Haven: Yale University Press, 1979.

Gledhill, Christine, ed. *Women and Melodrama*. Forthcoming. London: British Film Institute, 1986.

Haskell, Molly. *From Reverence to Rape: The Treatment of Women in the Movies*. New York: Penguin Books, 1974.

Hobson, Dorothy. "Housewives and the Mass Media." In *Culture, Media, Language*. Ed. Stuart Hall et al. London: Hutchinson, 1980, pp. 105–114.

Holland, Norman N., and Leona F. Sherman. "Gothic Possibilities." *New Literary History* 8 (Winter 1977), pp. 279–294.

Howells, Coral Ann. *Love, Mystery and Misery: Feeling in Gothic Fiction*. London: Athlone Press, 1978.

Jacobs, Lea. "*Now Voyager*: Some Problems of Enunciation and Sexual Difference." *Camera Obscura* 7 (1981), pp. 89–109.

Jensen, Margaret. "Women and Romantic Fiction: A Case Study of Harlequin Enterprises, Romances, and Readers." Diss. McMaster University, 1980.

Johnston, Claire. "Myths of Women in the Cinema." In *Women and the Cinema: A Critical Anthology*. Ed. Karyn Kay and Gerald Peary. New York: E.P. Dutton, 1977, pp. 407–411.

———. ed. *Notes on Women's Cinema*. London: SEFT, 1973.

Kaplan, E. Ann. "The Case of the Missing Mother: Maternal Issues in Vidor's *Stella Dallas*." *Heresies* 16 (1983), pp. 81–85.

———. *Women and Film: Both Sides of the Camera*. New York and London: Methuen, 1983.

Kowalski, Rosemary Ribich. *Women and Film: A Bibliography*. Metuchen, New Jersey: Scarecrow Press, 1976.

Kuhn, Annette. "Women's Genres." *Screen* 25:1 (January-February 1984), pp. 18–28.

Light, Alison. "'Returning to Manderley'—Romance Fiction, Female Sexuality and Class." *Feminist Review* 16 (Summer 1984), pp. 7–25.

Lopate, Carol. "Daytime Television: You'll Never Want to Leave Home." *Feminist Studies* 3:3–4 (Spring-Summer 1976), pp. 69–82.

———. "Jackie!" In *Hearth and Home: Images of Women in the Mass Media*. Ed. Gaye Tuchman, Arlene Kaplan Daniels, and James Benet. New York: Oxford University Press, 1978, pp. 130–140.

Mann, Peter H. *A New Survey: The Facts about Romantic Fiction*. London: Mills and Boon, 1974.

———. *The Romantic Novel: A Survey of Reading Habits*. London: Mills and Boon, 1969.

Mattelart, Michele. "Women and the Cultural Industries." *Media, Culture and Society* 4:2 (April 1982), pp. 133–151.

Miner, Madonne M. *Insatiable Appetites: Twentieth Century American Women's Best Sellers*. Westport, CT: Greenwood Press, 1984.

Modleski, Tanya. "The Disappearing Act: A Study of Harlequin Romances." *Signs* 5 (Spring 1980), pp. 435–438.

———. "Femininity as Mas(s)querade: A Feminist Critique of Mass Culture Theory." In *High Theory/Low Culture*. Ed. Colin McCabe. Manchester: University of Manchester Press, 1986.

———. *Loving With a Vengeance: Mass-Produced Fantasies for Women*. Hamden, CT: Archon Books, 1982.

———. "Never to Be Thirty-Six Years Old: *Rebecca* as Female Oedipal Drama." *Wide Angle* 5:1 (1982), pp. 34–41.

———. "The Rhythms of Reception: Daytime Television and Women's Work." In *Regarding Television*. Ed. E. Ann Kaplan. Los Angeles: University Publications of America, 1983, pp. 67–75.

———. "The Search for Tomorrow in Today's Soap Operas: Notes on a Feminine Narrative Form." *Film Quarterly* 33:1 (Fall 1979), pp. 12–21.

Mussell, Kay J. "Beautiful and Damned: The Sexual Woman in Gothic Fiction." *Journal of Popular Culture* 9:1 (Summer 1975), pp. 84–89.

———. "Romantic Fiction." In *The Handbook of American Popular Culture Volume II*. Ed. Thomas Ingi. Westport, CT: Greenwood Press, 1980, pp. 317–344.

Papashivly, Helen White. *All the Happy Endings: A Study of the Domestic Novel in America, the Women Who Wrote It, the Women Who Read It, in the Nineteenth Century*. New York: Harper and Brothers, 1956.

Perebinossoff, Philippe. "What Does a Kiss Mean? The Love Comic Formula and the Creation of the Ideal Teen-Age Girl." *Journal of Popular Culture* 8:4 (Spring 1975), pp. 825–835.

Porter, Dennis. "Soap Time: Thoughts on a Commodity Art Form." In *Television: The Critical View*. Ed. Horace Newcomb. New York and Oxford: Oxford University Press, 1982, pp. 122–131.

Rabine, Leslie. *Reading the Romantic Heroine: Text, History, Ideology*. Ann Arbor: University of Michigan Press, 1986.

Radner, Rebecca. "You're Being Paged Loudly in the Kitchen: Teen-Age Literature of the Forties and Fifties." *Journal of Popular Culture* 11:4 (Spring 1978), pp. 789–799.

Radway, Janice A. "Phenomenology, Linguistics, and Popular Literature." *Journal of Popular Culture* 12:1 (Summer 1978), pp. 88–98.

———. *Reading the Romance: Women, Patriarchy and Popular Literature*. Chapel Hill and London: University of North Carolina Press, 1984.

———. "The Utopian Impulse in Popular Literature: Gothic Romances and 'Feminist Protest'." *American Quarterly* 33 (Summer 1981), pp. 140–162.

———. "Women Read the Romance: The Interaction of Text and Context." *Feminist Studies* 9:1 (Spring 1983), pp. 53–78.

Renov, Michael. "Hollywood's Wartime Woman: A Study of Historical/Ideological Determination." Diss. University of California, Los Angeles, 1982.

Rosen, Marjorie. *Popcorn Venus: Women, Movies, and the American Dream*. New York: Coward, McCann and Geoghegan, 1972.

Rouse, Morleen Getz. "Daytime Radio Programming for the Homemaker, 1926–1956." *Journal of Popular Culture* 12:2 (Fall 1979), pp. 315–327.

Russ, Joanna. "Somebody's Trying to Kill Me and I Think It's My Husband: The Modern Gothic." *Journal of Popular Culture* 6:4 (Spring 1973), pp. 666–691.

Seiter, Ellen. "Promise and Contradiction: The Daytime Television Serials." *Film Reader* 5 (Winter 1982), pp. 150–153.

————. "The Promise of Melodrama: Recent Women's Films and Soap Operas." Diss. Northwestern University, 1981.

Showalter, Elaine. *A Literature of Their Own.* Princeton: Princeton University Press, 1977.

Snitow, Ann Barr. "Mass Market Romance: Pornography for Women Is Different." *Radical History Review* 20 (Spring-Summer 1979), pp. 141–161.

Swanson, Gillian. "*Dallas* Part I." *Framework* 14 (Spring 1981), pp. 32–35.

————. "*Dallas* Part II." *Framework* 15-16-17 (Summer 1981), pp. 81–85.

Tegler, Patricia. "The Daytime Serial: A Bibliography of Scholarly Writings 1943–1981." *Journal of Popular Culture* 16 (Winter 1982). Reprinted in *Life on Daytime Television: Tuning-In American Serial Drama.* Ed. Mary Cassata and Thomas Skill. Norwood, NJ: Ablex, 1983, pp. 187–196.

Thomas, Sari. "The Relationship Between Daytime Serials and Their Viewers." Diss. University of Pennsylvania, 1977.

Tompkins, Jane. *Sensational Designs: The Cultural Work of American Fiction, 1790–1860.* New York: Oxford, 1985.

Viviana, Christian. " 'Who Is Without Sin?' The Maternal Melodrama in American Film, 1930–1939." *Wide Angle* 4:2 (1980), pp. 4–17.

Waldman, Diane. " 'At Last I Can Tell It to Someone!': Feminine Point of View and Subjectivity in the Gothic Romance Film of the 1940's." *Cinema Journal* 23:2 (Winter 1984), pp. 29–40.

————. "Horror and Domesticity: The Modern Gothic Romance Film of the 1940's." Diss. University of Wisconsin, Madison, 1981.

Weibel, Kathryn. *Mirror Mirror: Images of Women Reflected in Popular Culture.* Garden City: Doubleday Anchor Press, 1977.

Williams, Linda. " 'Something Else Besides a Mother': *Stella Dallas* and the Maternal Melodrama." *Cinema Journal* 24:1 (Fall 1984), pp. 2–27.

Yeck, Joanne Louise. "The Woman's Film at Warner Brothers, 1935–1950." Diss. University of Southern California, 1982.

Writing the History of Women

The histories of women included here all hinge upon the doctrine of two spheres—the division between the private space of the family and the public space of the market. All of these histories variously engage a historiographical problem—namely, how to write the history of women and their social function in capitalist formations. Since there is no consensus as to how women's joint functions within the home and the marketplace can best be conceptualized, these histories approach the problem through a variety of methods and theoretical frameworks. Included are economic and labor histories, social histories, histories of representation, and biographical histories. In addition, we have devoted considerable attention to histories of the home and the family which have contributed both to the development of historiographical models and to our understanding of women's place in the private (libidinal) economies of the family and the public (market) economies of capitalist society.

Andrews, William D., and Deborah C. Andrews. "Technology and the Housewife in Nineteenth-Century America." *Women's Studies* 2:1 (1974), pp. 309–328.

Aries, Phillipe. *Centuries of Childhood: A Social History of Family Life.* Trans. Robert Baldick. New York: Vintage Books, 1962.

———. "The Family and the City in the Old World and the New." In *Changing Images of the Family.* Ed. Virginia Tufte and Barbara Meyerhoff. New Haven and London: Yale University Press, 1979, pp. 29–41.

Beauvoir, Simone de. *The Second Sex.* Trans. and Ed. H.M. Parshley. New York: Knopf, 1953.

Beecher, Catharine E., and Harriet Beecher Stowe. *The American Woman's Home: or Principles of Domestic Science.* 1869. Hartford: Stowe-Day Foundation, 1975.

Berch, Bettina. "Scientific Management in the Home: The Empress's New Clothes." *Journal of American Culture* 3:3 (Fall 1980), pp. 440–445.

Berk, Richard A. *Labor and Leisure at Home: Content and Organization of the Household Day.* Beverly Hills: Sage, 1975.

The Black Family and the Black Woman: A Bibliography. Bloomington: Prepared by the library staff and the Afro-American Studies Department, Indiana University, 1972.

Branca, Patricia. *Silent Sisterhood: Middle-Class Women in the Victorian Home.* Pittsburgh: Carnegie-Mellon University Press, 1975.

Brownmiller, Susan. *Femininity.* New York: Simon and Schuster, 1984.

Carrell, Kimberley W. "The Industrial Revolution Comes to the Home: Kitchen Design Reform and Middle-Class Women." *Journal of American Culture* 2:3 (Fall 1979), pp. 488–499.

Carroll, Berenice A., ed. *Liberating Women's History: Theoretical and Critical Essays.* Urbana, Chicago, and London: University of Illinois Press, 1976.

Chafe, William H. *The American Woman: Her Changing Social, Economic, and Political Roles, 1920–1970.* New York: Oxford University Press, 1972.

———. *Women and Equality: Changing Patterns in American Culture.* New York: Oxford University Press, 1977.

Cohn, Jan. *The Palace or the Poorhouse: The American House as Cultural Symbol.* East Lansing: Michigan State University Press, 1979.

Cott, Nancy. *The Bonds of Womanhood: Woman's Sphere in New England, 1780–1835.* New Haven: Yale University Press, 1977.

Cowan, Ruth Schwartz. "A Case Study of Technological and Social Change: The Washing Machine and the Working Wife." In *Clio's Consciousness Raised: New Perspectives on the History of Women.* Ed. Mary S. Hartman and Lois Banner. New York: Octagon Books, 1976, pp. 245–253.

———. "The 'Industrial Revolution' in the Home: Household Technology and Social Change in the Twentieth Century." *Technology and Culture* 17 (January 1976), pp. 1–23.

———. *More Work for Mother: The Ironies of Household Technology from the Open Hearth to the Microwave.* New York: Basic Books, 1983.

Degler, Carl N. *At Odds: Women and the Family in America from the Revolution to the Present.* New York: Oxford University Press, 1980

——— . *Women and the Family in the Past Before Us: Contemporary Historical Writing in the United States*. Ed. Michael Kaminen. Ithaca and London: Cornell University Press, 1980.

Demos, Jon. "Images of the American Family, Then and Now." In *Changing Images of the Family*. Ed. Virginia Tufte and Barbara Meyerhoff. New Haven and London: Yale University Press, 1979, pp. 43–60.

Donzelot, Jacques. *The Policing of Families*. New York: Pantheon Books, 1979.

Douglas, George H. *Women of the 20s*. Dallas: Saybrook, 1986.

Ehrenreich, Barbara, and Deirdre English. *Complaints and Disorders: The Sexual Politics of Sickness*. Old Westbury, New York: The Feminist Press, 1973.

——— . *For Her Own Good: 150 Years of Experts' Advice to Women*. Garden City, New York: Anchor Press, 1978.

——— . "The Manufacture of Housework." *Socialist Revolution* 5 (October-December 1975), pp. 5–40.

——— . *Witches, Midwives and Nurses*. Old Westbury, NY: The Feminist Press, 1973.

Fass, Paula S. *The Damned and the Beautiful: American Youth in the 1920s*. New York: Oxford University Press, 1977.

Folbre, Nancy. "Exploitation Comes Home: A Critique of the Marxian Theory of Family Labor." *Cambridge Journal of Economics* (1982), pp. 317–329.

Foucault, Michel. *The History of Sexuality Volume I: An Introduction*. Trans. Robert Hurley. New York: Vintage Books, 1980.

Fox-Genovese, Elizabeth. "Placing Women's History in History." *New Left Review* 133 (May-June 1982), pp. 5–29.

Fraser, Nancy. "What's Critical About Critical Theory? The Case of Habermas and Gender." *New Germand Critique* 35 (Spring-Summer 1985), pp. 97–132.

Friedman, Jean E., and William G. Shade, eds. *Our American Sisters: Women in American Life and Thought*. 2nd ed. Boston: Allyn and Bacon, 1976.

Garnsey, E. "Women's Work and Theories of Class Stratification." *Sociology* 12:2 (1978), pp. 223–244.

Gay, Peter. *The Bourgeois Experience, Victoria to Freud: Education of the Senses Volume I*. New York and Oxford: Oxford University Press, 1984.

Gilman, Charlotte Perkins. *The Home: Its Work and Influence*. 1903. Urbana: University of Illinois Press, 1972.

——— . *Woman and Economics: The Economic Factor Between Men and Women as a Factor in Social Evolution*. 1898. New York: Source Book Press, 1970.

Gordan, Linda. "What Should Women's Historians Do: Politics, Social Theory, and Women's History." *Marxist Perspectives* 1:3 (Fall 1978), pp. 128–137.

Gorham, Deborah. *The Victorian Girl and the Feminine Ideal*. Bloomington: Indiana University Press, 1982.

Grant, Mary H. "Domestic Experience and Feminist Theory: The Case of Julia Ward Howe." In *Woman's Being, Woman's Place: Female Identity and Vocation in American History*. Ed. Mary Kelley. Boston: G.K. Hall & Co., 1979, pp. 220–232.

Greene, Harvey. *The Light of the Home: An Intimate View of the Lives of Women in Victorian America*. New York: Pantheon, 1983.

Halftunen, Karen. *Confidence Men and Painted Women: A Study of Middle-Class Culture in America, 1830–1870*. New Haven and London: Yale University Press, 1982.

Hareven, Tamara. "Modernization and Family History: Perspectives on Social Change." *Signs* 2:1 (Fall 1976), pp. 190–206.

Harris, Alice Kessler. "Independence and Virtue in the Lives of Wage-Earning Women: The United States, 1870–1930." In *Women in Culture and Politics: A Century of Change.* Ed. Judith Friedlander et al. Bloomington: University of Indiana, 1986, pp. 3–17.

Harrison, Cynthia. *Women in American History: A Bibliography.* Santa Barbara, CA: American Bibliographical Center–Clio Press, 1979.

Hartman, Mary S., and Lois Banner, eds. *Clio's Consciousness Raised: New Perspectives on the History of Women.* New York: Octagon Books, 1976.

Hartmann, Heidi. "Capitalism and Women's Work in the Home 1900–1930." Diss. Yale University, 1974.

―――. "The Family as the Locus of Gender, Class and Political Struggle: The Example of Housework." *Signs* 6 (Spring 1981), pp. 366–394.

Hayden, Dolores. "Charlotte Perkins Gilman and the Kitchenless House." *Radical History Review* 21 (Fall 1979), pp. 225–247.

―――. *The Grand Domestic Revolution: A History of Feminist Designs for American Homes, Neighborhoods, and Cities.* Cambridge: MIT Press, 1981.

―――. *Redesigning the American Dream: The Future of Housing, Work, and Family Life.* New York: W.W. Norton, 1984.

Hobson, D. "Housewives: Isolation as Oppression." In *Women Take Issue.* Ed. Women's Study Group, Centre for Contemporary Cultural Studies. London: Hutchinson, 1978, pp. 79–95.

Howe, Louise Kapp. *Pink-Collar Workers: Inside the World of Women's Work.* New York: Putnam. 1977.

Jeffreys, Sheila. *The Spinster and Her Enemies: Feminism and Sexuality 1880–1930.* London, Boston, and Henley: Pandora Press, 1985.

Jenkins, William D. "Housewifery and Motherhood: The Question of Role Change in the Progressive Era." In *Woman's Being, Woman's Place: Female Identity and Vocation in American History.* Ed. Mary Kelley. Boston: G.K. Hall & Co., 1979, pp. 142–153.

Jones, Jacqueline. *Labor of Love, Labor of Sorrow: Black Women, Work, and the Family from Slavery to the Present.* New York: Basic Books, 1985.

Kelley, Mary. "At War With Herself: Harriet Beecher Stowe as Woman in Conflict within the Home." In *Woman's Being, Woman's Place: Female Identity and Vocation in American History.* Ed. Mary Kelley. Boston: G.K. Hall & Co., 1979.

Kelly, Joan. *Women, History and Theory: The Essays of Joan Kelly.* Chicago: University of Chicago Press, 1984.

Kennedy, Susan Estabrook. *If All We Did Was to Weep at Home: A History of White Working-Class Women in America.* Bloomington: Indiana University Press, 1979.

Kovel, Joel. "Rationalization and the Family." *Telos* 37 (Fall 1978), pp. 5–21.

Kunzle, David. "Dress Reform as Antifeminism: A Response to Helene E. Robert's 'The Exquisite Slave'." *Signs* 2 (Spring 1977), pp. 570–579.

―――. *Fashion and Fetishism: A Social History of the Corset, Tight-Lacing and Other Forms of Body Sculpture in the West.* Totowa, NJ: Rowman and Littlefield, 1980.

Lasch, Christopher. *Haven in a Heartless World: The Family Besieged.* New York: Basic Books, 1977.

———. "Woman as Alien." In *Our American Sisters: Women in American Life and Thought*. Ed. Jean E. Friedman and William G. Shade. 1st ed. Boston: Allyn and Bacon, 1973, pp. 168–186.

Laslett, Barbara. "The Family as a Public and Private Institution: An Historical Perspective." *Journal of Marriage and the Family* 35 (August 1973), pp. 480–492.

Lee, Antoinette. "Party Walls and Private Lives: Aspects of a Railway Suburb." *Women's Studies* 3:3 (1976), pp. 251–277.

Lerner, Gerda. *The Majority Finds Its Past: Placing Women in History*. New York: Oxford University Press, 1979.

Matthei, Julie A. *An Economic History of Women in America: Women's Work, the Sexual Division of Labor and the Development of Capitalism*. New York: Schocken Books, 1982.

McGovern, James R. "The American Woman's Pre–World War I Freedom in Manners and Morals." In *Our American Sisters: Women in American Life and Thought*. Ed. Jean E. Freidman and William G. Shade. 2nd ed. Boston: Allyn and Bacon, 1976, pp. 345–365.

Milkman, Ruth. "Redefining 'Women's Work': The Sexual Division of Labor in the Auto Industry During World War II." *Feminist Studies* 8:2 (Summer 1982), pp. 336–372.

Molyneux, Maxine. "Beyond the Domestic Labour Debate." *New Left Review* 116 (July-August 1979), pp. 3–28.

Oakley, Ann. *Woman's Work: The Housewife, Past and Present*. New York: Pantheon Books, 1975.

Poster, Mark. *Critical Theory of the Family*. New York: Seabury Press, 1978.

Rapp, Rayna, and Ellen Ross. "The Twenties' Backlash: Compulsory Heterosexuality, the Consumer Family, and the Waning of Feminism." In *Class, Race, and Sex: The Dynamics of Control*. Ed. Amy Swerdlow and Hannah Lessinger. Boston: G.K. Hall, 1983, pp. 93–107.

Roberts, Helene E. "The Exquisite Slave: The Role of Clothes in the Making of the Victorian Woman." *Signs* 2:3 (Spring 1977), pp. 554–569.

Robinson, Lillian. *Sex, Class and Culture*. Bloomington: Indiana University Press, 1978.

Rollins, Judith. *Between Women: Domestics and Their Employers*. Philadephia: Temple University Press, 1985.

Rothman, Sheila M. *Woman's Proper Place: A History of Changing Ideals and Practices, 1870 to the Present*. New York: Basic Books, 1978.

Rowbotham, Sheila. *Woman's Consciousness, Man's World*. Harmondsworth and Middlesex: Penguin Books Ltd., 1973.

Rubin, Lillian Breslow. *Worlds of Pain: Life in the Working-Class Family*. New York: Basic Books, 1976.

Rupp, Leila. *Mobilizing Women for War: German and American Propaganda, 1939–1945*. Princeton: Princeton University Press, 1978

Ryan, Mary P. *Womanhood in America: From Colonial Times to the Present*. New York: New Viewpoints, 1975.

Saegert, Susan. "Masculine Cities and Feminine Suburbs: Polarized Ideas, Contradictory Realities." *Signs* 5:3, Supplement (Spring 1980), pp. S96–S111.

Sawhill, Isabel V. "Economic Perspectives on the Family." *Daedalus* 106:2 (Spring 1977), pp. 115–126.

Schofield, Ann. "Rebel Girls and Union Maids: The Woman Question in the Journals of the AFL and IWW, 1905–1920." *Feminist Studies* 9:2 (Summer 1983), pp. 335–358.

Sennett, Richard. *The Fall of Public Man.* New York: Knopf. 1978.

Shorter, Edward. *The Making of the Modern Family.* New York: Basic Books, 1975.

Sklar, Kathryn Kish. *Catherine Beecher: A Study in American Domesticity.* New York: Norton, 1976.

————, ed. *Readings in the Social History of American Women: Family, Work, and Collectives 1600–1820.* Los Angeles: Department of History, University of California, Los Angeles, 1976.

Skolnick, Arlene. "Public Images, Private Realities: The American Family in Popular Culture and Social Science." In *Changing Images of the Family.* Ed. Virginia Tufte and Barbara Meyerhoff. New Haven and London: Yale University Press, 1979, pp. 297–315.

Sokoloff, Natalie J. *Between Money and Love: The Dialectics of Women's Home and Market Work.* New York: Praeger, 1980.

Sprigg, June. *Domestic Beings.* New York: Knopf, 1984.

Steele, Victoria. *Fashion and Eroticism: Ideals of Feminine Beauty from the Victorian Era to the Jazz Age.* New York: Oxford University Press, 1985.

Strasser, Susan. "Mistress and Maid, Employer and Employee: Domestic Service Reform in the United States, 1897–1920." *Marxist Perspectives* 1:3 (Fall 1978), pp. 52–67.

————. *Never Done: A History of American Housework.* New York: Pantheon Books, 1982.

Straub, Eleanor Ferguson. "Government Policy Toward Civilian Women During World War II." Diss. Emory University, 1973.

Tentler, Leslie Woodcock. *Wage-Earning Women: Industrial Work and Family Life in the United States, 1900–1930.* New York: Oxford University Press, 1979.

Tilly, Louise, A., and Joan W. Scott. *Women, Work, and the Family.* New York: Holt, Rinehart and Winston, 1978.

Trey, J.E. "Women in the War Economy—World War II." *Review of Radical Political Economics* 4 (July 1972), pp. 41–57.

Wandersee, Winnifred D. *Women's Work and Family Values, 1920–1940.* Cambridge: Harvard University Press, 1981.

Welter, Barbara. "The Cult of True Womanhood, 1820–1860." *American Quarterly* 18 (Summer 1966), pp. 151–174.

Wertheimer, Barbara Mayer. *We Were There: The Story of Working Women in America* New York: Pantheon Books, 1977.

Women's Studies Group, Centre for Contemporary Cultural Studies. *Women Take Issue.* London: Hutchinson, 1978.

Wright, Gwendolyn. *Building the Dream: A Social History of Housing in America.* New York: Pantheon Books, 1981.

Zaretsky, Eli. *Capitalism, The Family and Personal Life.* New York and Cambridge: Harper & Row, 1976.

Quar. Rev. of Film & Video, Vol. 11, pp. 107–112
Reprints available directly from the publisher
Photocopying permitted by license only

Harwood Academic Publishers, 1989
Printed in the United States of America

Review Essay

The Riddle of the Reader in Mass-Produced 'Women's Fiction'

Lynn Spigel

Robert C. Allen. *Speaking of Soap Operas*. Chapel Hill and London: University of North Carolina Press, 1985. 245 pp. $9.95 paper.

Janice A. Radway. *Reading the Romance: Women, Patriarchy and Popular Literature*. Chapel Hill and London: University of North Carolina Press, 1985. 274 pp. $7.95 paper.

Until relatively recent years, the study of mass culture for women has been one of the most underdeveloped fields of critical investigation. Undoubtedly, the litany of aesthetic devaluations applied to mass art in general and especially to "women's weepies" and "soap operas" has contributed to the scarcity of literature. Against this tradition of aesthetic hierarchies, feminist critics are in the process of reconceptualizing the relationship between mass-produced texts and the large number of women to whom they appeal. It is precisely this interest in reader-text relations which motivates Robert C. Allen's *Speaking of Soap Operas* and Janice A. Radway's *Reading the Romance: Women, Patriarchy and Popular Literature*. Dealing respectively with broadcast soap operas (both radio and television) and contemporary mass-produced romance novels, Allen and Radway share a sense of dissatisfaction with the way in which the female reader has been understood and suggest alternative approaches.

Speaking of Soap Operas begins with an incisive reassessment of the way in which soap operas and their audiences have been conceptualized. In particular, Allen reconsiders American Mass Communications, which is the dominant paradigm through which broadcast narratives and audiences are studied. He argues that Mass Communications is based upon empiricist assumptions which, when applied to complex cultural systems, lead to extremely limited knowledge. Most significant to Allen is that empiricism lacks a theory of causality and, therefore, cannot explain adequately the mechanisms responsible for mass-produced texts and their reception. As an alternative, he turns to the critical frameworks of literary and film studies and uses multiple strategies of investigation, including narrative and reception theory as well as institutional and historical analysis.

Allen begins by laying out a set of abstract governing laws. In part, this is a description of the economic imperatives of soap opera production. But it is also

LYNN SPIGEL *is an assistant professor of Communication Arts at the University of Wisconsin-Madison, and author of the forthcoming book,* Installing the Television Set.

what Allen calls a "reader-oriented poetics" which attempts to establish the basic principles upon which the soap opera narrative and its reception are based. Using structural linguistics, semiotics, and reception theory, Allen characterizes the soap opera as a text which encourages multiple interpretations. As he writes, "The soap opera represents an 'over-coded' narrative form in which characters and relationships are endowed with pluri-significative possibilities. . ." (p. 94).

As Allen admits, his poetics is based upon a rather eclectic group of sources (including, for example, Jonathan Culler, Umberto Eco, and Wolfgang Iser). This allows Allen to look at the soap opera from a variety of theoretical perspectives (and he is careful to explain each one). But it does at times lead to confusion, especially in terms of the way in which Allen characterizes the reader-text relationship. On the one hand, he uses a semiological approach. He argues that the soap opera is what Eco calls an "open text," a text which contains multiple interpretive strategies (or codes) which allow for a range of possible readings. As Allen explains it, this model presupposes that readings are largely regulated by the text. "The notion of codes helps us to recognize that the pluri-signification of the soap opera is not achieved willy-nilly but via certain generalizable pathways" (p. 84). On the other hand, he uses Iser's phenomenological approach which emphasizes the reader's active engagement in the interpretive process. Here he argues that the soap opera narrative is organized around "syntagmatic gaps," or breaks between narrative segments. These gaps further engender multiple meanings because they open up a space for imaginative play. "It is precisely at these places where the textual 'pavement' is broken that the reader's active involvement is most clearly seen. What the text leaves unsaid is, nevertheless, made to signify within the imagination of the reader" (p. 78). While a semiological analysis of codes and a phenomenological analysis of the act of reading are not necessarily incompatible, Allen does not sufficiently explain the ways in which they do and do not fit together. Ultimately, we are left with a question of determinations. To what extent are the soap opera's multiple meanings determined by the text's instructions for interpretation, and to what extent is this "pluri-signification" achieved through the reader's active participation?[1]

While Allen never solves this riddle, his emphasis upon multiple interpretations is important for several reasons. First, it reverses the widely held belief that mass-produced "formula" art contains clear-cut messages which are read in the same way by all readers. Second, it is a response to feminist soap opera critics, especially in terms of what has been said about the female reader. Among the most influential of these critics is Tania Modleski, who argues that the soap opera offers a specifically female position from which to read. She claims that by, for example, including numerous characters with whom to identify and by denying absolute closure, the soap opera positions its reader as an "ideal mother" who must empathize with all her children and whose life in the home is based upon continual expectation of events to come.[2] For Allen, this association of the soap opera reader with the housewife/mother is too restrictive because, as he argues, the soap opera narrative "allows for a variety of responses from a number of different readerships" (p. 94).

As Allen acknowledges, his textual analysis which does not account for a female reader cannot explain the soap opera's overwhelmingly female audience. However, I would argue that this is, to a large degree, a positive move which adds important qualifications to Modleski's work. For as Allen suggests, analyses of the female subject position "inscribed" in the text ignore historical variations in the production and reception of soap operas. Ultimately, then, Allen does not want to derive a female reader through methods of textual analysis alone. Rather, he explains the soap opera's female audience by turning to historical analysis.

Indeed, Allen's historical analysis is the most intriguing part of the book. Not only does he provide an institutional history, but he also offers a reception history. As Allen intends it, his reception history is a preliminary outline which suggests key questions for future research. Here, for example, Allen considers the history of "women's fiction," and in particular the nineteenth-century domestic novel, which he claims provided a "horizon of expectations" against which radio soap operas were read. In addition, he speaks at length about changes in the soap opera's textual system and the subject positions it has offered to readers. He claims that the strong presence of an extradiegetic narrator in the radio soap opera led to a rather didactic text in which female readers were given a limited set of perspectives on the social world. In the transition from radio to television, the narrator figure disappeared, and the text became more open to a variety of perspectives and meanings.

Even in its tentative nature, Allen's reception history is an important contribution because it suggests that the reader-text relationship changes over time and that these changes should form a major focus for the study of mass-produced texts for women. However, as he admits, this project leaves us with a nagging question. How is it possible to specify the ways in which real readers in the past actually interpreted soap operas?

It is precisely this interest in the real reader which Radway takes up in *Reading the Romance*. The book asks why women read mass-produced romances, what satisfactions they obtain and how they understand these novels—questions which in recent years have become central to feminist critics. Radway argues that her fellow critics have been overly subjective and idiosyncratic because they have typically dismissed the "explanations of the romance readers themselves in order to privilege [their] reading of the novel and [their] explanation for why it is read. . ." (p. 5). *Reading the Romance* is in large part a reply to this problem, taking as its point of departure a group of women who read romances.

Methodologically the book is especially interesting because Radway attempts to bridge the gulf between relatively distinct approaches to mass culture. She combines audience research techniques of the social sciences with the critical methods used in literary and film studies (including narrative theory, reception theory, and psychoanalysis). It should be pointed out, however, that the relationship between social scientific approaches and those of critical studies is not a simple matter of grafting one onto the other. These approaches have traditionally asked very different kinds of questions, and it is not at all obvious, for example, what the conscious responses of an audience can say about the way in which meaning arises in the reading process. Thus, *Reading the Romance* inserts itself at the as yet tentative intersection of two distinct paradigms of study.

Radway begins with a historical analysis of book publishing in America, emphasizing the institutional changes in production and distribution which frame the contemporary romance novel market. Since, Radway argues, critics tend to ignore the publishing institution itself, they often assume that these novels are popular because they immediately reflect the social world and female desire in that world.

Against this reflection model, Radway argues that there is an imperfect fit between female desires and the books produced by the industry. Moreover, she shows that the popularity of romance novels is as much a function of industrial strategies (advertising, market research, commodity packaging, etc.) as it is a function of the genre's ability to speak to readers' concerns.

From this analysis of the romance novel market, Radway moves to a case study of forty-two female romance novel readers in Smithton, Pennsylvania, a relatively affluent suburban community. In selecting this sample she aligns herself much more with an anthropological approach than she does with the basic tenets of empiricist mass communications research. As she admits, these women do not necessarily comprise a representative sample of romance novel readers. This neglect of empiricist methods does not, however, represent a failure to be scientifically rigorous because Radway is not really attempting to make generalizable claims about romance readers. Instead, she concentrates upon the very localized relations of reception and presents a portrait of the everyday life of the typical Smithton romance reader.[3] By focusing on the experiences of the reader, Radway wants to show the belief systems which frame these women's lives, for "when analysis proceeds from within the belief system actually brought to bear on the text by its readers, the analytical interpretation of the meaning of a character's behavior is more likely to coincide with that meaning as it is constructed and understood by the readers themselves" (p. 78).

This interest in belief systems often leads to extremely provocative methods of analysis. Perhaps the most valuable model Radway proposes comes with her examination of "ideal" and "failed" romances. Through her audience survey questions, Radway finds that the Smithton women like certain books and detest others. Although this might seem strikingly obvious, most mass-culture critics, as Radway explains, assume that category novels are endless repetitions of the same story and, therefore, can be analyzed through methods of random sampling. In opposition to this, Radway attempts to understand the genre as the reader group does by analyzing their favorite and least preferred novels. Using Propp along with Will Wright's inflection of social action, Radway shows the essential narrative functions and character types in the romance novel. Among the basic requirements she finds the developing love relationship between a heroine and a hero as well as a happy ending. Radway then compares her findings to audience surveys which indicate that the Smithton women often prefer novels that have the narrative structure and character types which her analysis suggests.

Radway's investigation of the "act of reading" is also provocative. Here she argues that while culture critics proceed on the basis of narrative interpretation, little attention is given to the reader's decision to actively engage the text. Radway presents detailed conversations among the group concerning the reasons they read romances. From these conversations she deduces two primary motivations— escape and instruction. Romance novels allow these women to disengage themselves from their everyday chores and enter a realm of fantasy. At the same time, the readers claim that they learn from romances because the novels give information about far-away places, information which they take to be accurate. And interestingly, as Radway points out, the women do not have a problem in accepting the plot as fantasy on the one hand and the setting as real on the other hand.

Perhaps this analysis of the reading act is convincing because it relies on the interpretations of the readers themselves. But Radway is much less successful when she attempts to disclose the unconscious motivations behind the act of reading. Here she uses Nancy Chodorow's *Reproduction of Mothering* to suggest that romance reading is a "compensatory act" based on the women's need to find a "self-in-relation." Since women in their adult lives cannot find the nurturance they experienced with their mothers, they seek support via compensation. In Chodorow's terms this "self-in-relation" is achieved by becoming a mother, by caring for others. But in Radway's terms the reading of romance novels which depict a developing love relationship can itself compensate (although only temporarily) for the woman's need for nurturance. Whether or not we agree with Chodorow's theory, Radway's application is problematic because of the curious position she adopts. In trying to correlate the reader's conscious reactions with her own interpretations of unconscious motivations, Radway is backed into the corner of the psychiatrist's office. Rather than presenting an analysis of the way in which desire arises in the reader-text relationship, Radway psychologizes the reader's life in a very generalized fashion. This, I would argue, is the primary problem at stake in the attempt to relate audience research to a critical perspective on subjectivity and narrativity. How can we make the transition from conscious reactions to the unconscious and discursive relations between reader and text?

Radway does attempt to deal with this question. In keeping with her overall interest in belief systems, she tries to specify the way in which the Smithton readers perceive language in the romance novel and the way in which this perception affects interpretations. Through audience research and her own narrative analysis, she suggests that the readers take this language to be referential. As she writes, "They treat that language . . . as if it simply designated a world entirely congruent or continuous with their own" (p. 191). She then goes on to argue that the novels provide readers with a mythic fantasy, a fantasy laden with the patriarchal values of the romantic couple, marriage, and female self-sacrifice. Since, she claims, the readers believe that language refers to the real world, this patriarchal fantasy itself appears to be real. Thus, even while the women use these novels to escape from their everyday lives in the nuclear family, romances reinforce those oppressive conditions.

While this analysis suggests the need to take readers' perceptions into account, it makes rather rash assumptions. Why does Radway assume that it is possible to analyze language from the point of view of the readers' conscious perceptions? Radway almost entirely ignores the way in which language itself mobilizes desire and pleasure in the reading process (and her almost total neglect of language in her analysis of "ideal" and "failed" romances further suggests this problem). In Radway's account, it appears that language can only refer to desire (i.e., it refers to the fantasy content of the tale). Again, Radway's attempt to combine audience research with critical interpretation places her in a bind. For while it is possible to analyze conscious responses to language, it is far more difficult to understand how these responses relate to unconscious desire and pleasure in narrative.

In the space of this review I have not been able to convey fully the complexity of the tasks which Allen and Radway take on. By approaching the question of mass-produced fictions and their readers through a number of methods and theoretical perspectives, both authors offer a particularly rich analysis and suggest new directions for research. If not entirely successful, *Speaking of Soap Operas* and *Reading the Romance* are two of the most thoughtful considerations of the dynamics among mass cultural institutions, the texts they produce, and the large number of women to whom they appeal.

NOTES

1. This question of determinations is, of course, a complex problem which continues to vex narrative and reception theory. Allen often solves this problem by arguing that the text lays out instructions for meaning but that the reader can negotiate with the text. While this is a practical solution, it still does not explain how much freedom the reader actually has in interpreting the text, nor does the concept of negotiation, as Allen explains it, entirely match with the concept of active participation. For a good overview of theories of narrative and reception (including semiotics and phenomenology) see Susan Sulieman and Inge Crossman, eds., "Introduction: Varieties of Audience-Oriented Criticism," in *The Reader in the Text* (Princeton: Princeton University Press, 1980), pp. 3–45.
2. Tania Modleski, *Loving with a Vengeance: Mass-Produced Fantasies for Women* (New York: Methuen, 1982), pp. 85–109. See also her other works: "The Search for Tomorrow in Today's Soap Operas: Notes on a Feminine Narrative Form," *Film Quarterly* 33, no. 1 (1979), pp. 12–21, and "The Rhythms of Reception: Daytime Television and Women's Work," in *Regarding Television*, American Film Institute Monograph Series 2, ed. E. Ann Kaplan (Los Angeles: University Publications of America, 1983), pp. 67–75.
3. Much of this case study is devoted to one woman, a bookstore clerk and the author of a romance novel newsletter, who serves as an advisory critic for the group. This is coupled with more general readership surveys and conversations with the Smithton group.

Quar. Rev. of Film & Video, Vol. 11, pp. 113–115
Reprints available directly from the publisher
Photocopying permitted by license only

Harwood Academic Publishers, 1989
Printed in the United States of America

Review Essay

Harlequins, Gothics, and Soap Operas: Addressing Needs and Masking Fears

Jeanne Allen

Tania Modleski. *Loving with a Vengeance: Mass-Produced Fantasies for Women*. London and New York: Methuen, 1984. $15.00 cloth. $6.95 paper.

My pleasure in reading, rereading, and teaching *Loving with a Vengeance* is equally divided between the brilliance of its insight into the interaction between female readers and texts psychologically and the lucid and concise manner of its expression. On one level reading this book enriched my understanding of the place of "feminine popular narratives" in my own life: my choice of *The Turn of the Screw* and the film adaptation of it for a dissertation study of narrative ambiguity, my intrigue with *Days of Our Lives* since the summer I spent studying for comps, my mother's habitual viewing of *Dallas* reruns despite my father's equally habitual consternation and attempts to interrupt, or my sister's absorption in Harlequins, the great domestic disappearing act, the year before her divorce.

On another level, that of a professional academic, I was appreciative of the blend of intellectual analysis and commitment to quality of life experience that has attracted me to feminist criticism and to feminist women: not repressing strong feelings which absorb our attention but illuminating them with contextual richness, making connections between levels of social experience, rather than privileging one over the other. I agree with Judith Mayne's assessment of the book as the best contribution yet on the relation of women and popular culture; I think it still holds that position, although the way was well prepared by scholars such as Beatrice Hofstadter, John Cawelti, Kay Mussell, Ann Douglas, and more recently Joanna Russ and Carolyn Heilbrun, whose work Modleski incorporates to great advantage.

Modleski's ability to take the momentum of "the madwoman in the attic" strain of feminist literary criticism and to position it as clarifying the ancestors for these three mass culture forms—Harlequins, Gothics, and soap operas—while linking them to particular psychoanalytically illuminated types of experience is both a politically strategic and culturally provocative manner of offering a rationale for our interest. Bringing the growing literature of feminist criticism to bear on mass-produced culture aimed at women poses a number of issues about mass culture criticism and our attitudes toward it which Modleski must deal with initially.

Modleski's opening chapter and afterword are crucial and concise frames for her project, laying out the problem, her response, and manner of approach. The

JEANNE ALLEN teaches film, television, and mass culture at Temple University, Philadelphia, Pennsylvania 19122.

problem is the neglect of "feminine popular narratives" as a subject for critical analysis and the need to avoid a simple role reversal substitution of women for men in male hero genres. Modleski attributes this neglect to a perception of *heroism* as aggrandizement, viewed as unfeminine in our culture, and to a scorn for what is feminine, often expressed in hostility, dismissal, or flippant mockery.

Modleski seeks to correct this situation by arguing that the longevity and popularity of certain feminine genres evidence their ability to address real problems and tensions in women's lives. Her examination of narrative strategies in Harlequin romances, Gothic novels, and television soap operas reveals how women have managed to live in oppressive circumstances and go further, investing their situation with some degree of dignity. The notion of the utopian quality of mass culture is fundamental here. Modleski points out that feminists and readers of these forms of mass culture (are they different people?) can agree on the dissatisfactions of their situation; what they can't agree about is how to deal with them.

The ability of mass culture forms to address needs, mask fears, to disclose the contradictions within the answers to problems is the basis for taking it seriously. Modleski claims that mass culture is no less complex than high culture but because less transformation and distanciation of anxieties and wishes is operating, we can see how it maintains certain attitudes and behaviors more directly. If Carolyn Heilbrun is right that the only motivation for reaching women in capitalist patriarchy is to reach them as consumers (the brief period of courtship is perhaps another) then the products of these industries should be effective barometers.

Modleski shares with Janice Radway (*Reading the Romance*) a view of women's fiction as offering fulfillment in a manner impossible to act out: the compatibility and/or reduced polarity of gender is not advocated or explained but rather achieved by a *magical transformation* of the man or clarified as a misperception or misunderstanding on the part of the woman so that he can parent (i.e. *mother* after Chodorow and Dinnerstein) the woman/mother. When Modleski says that Marxists study the unconscious as structured by the family to understand why women prefer symbolic to real satisfactions (p. 29), I think the issue is less a preference for the symbolic than the fictional fraught with contradiction to the point that imitation outside the text is inconceivable.

The lucidity and concision of Modleski's prose is a particularly remarkable achievement in a field reknowned for the difficulty and jargon of some of its basic texts. Modleski's rhetoric is personably involved at moments in a way that is engaging without being distracting—almost an essayistic personality that marks the feminist mode of aiming not only for analytical rigor but at wisdom born of experience and caring. This is a significant part of the book's ability to attract and influence readers who may not share its political stance. A Marxist psychoanalytic feminist approach to mass culture is not every student's cup of tea. That undergraduates without a background in literary criticism can understand and respond to this book—something one cannot always say of feminist film criticism and theory—only validates some of the best counsel I heard in graduate school: "If you cannot explain your ideas clearly to a bright undergraduate, you don't really know or understand them very well."

But *Loving with a Vengeance* is not a particularly theoretical work; it is a piece of mass culture criticism which links Marxism and psychoanalysis without much direct discussion of how best that can be done and why. It doesn't, for example, explain its position with regard to the critical reaction against Althusser, the divisions between political economy-oriented Marxists and the more "autonomous ideology" Marxists. "Rejecting the notion of 'false consciousness' many Marxists have turned to a study of the unconscious as it is structured in and by the family" (p. 29). But the premises of the psychoanalytic construction of the self and the presentation of family as a historical economic institution are not as compatible as Modleski's linkages would seem to make them.

As Annette Kuhn points out, the difficulties of synthesizing contextual and psychoanalytic analysis are considerable. In her chapter on Gothics, Modleski's examination of inequitable power relations between parents reinforces psychoanalytic ahistoricity by assuring a fixed or static relation common to all social classes and historical periods. Not everything can be explained in one book, but reference to the growing literature on family would contextualize her explanation as would even general works like Zaretsky's *Capitalism, Family and Personal Life*. Ilene Philipson's "Heterosexual Antagonisms and the Politics of Mothering" (*Socialist Review* #66, Vol. 12, No. 6 (Nov.–Dec. 1982): 55–77), for example, would make "family" a more specific and culturally constructed entity than Modleski assumes. Philipson's study of middle-class family life in the 1950s interprets the conclusions of her study in terms of the work of Nancy Chodorow and others in a way useful to Modleski's identification of the revival of Gothic popularity and the gaslight film as a reaction to the World War II experience of women's independence (p. 21). I'm not suggesting that Modleski needed to perform survey research like Philipson or undertake Geertzian ethnographies like Radway, but that we need to go further in investigating capitalism's interest in consumerizing aspirations favorable to its maintenance—to consider the specifics of class, nationality, and historical period. Discussions of the domineering mother, apart from post–World War II demographics and employment patterns, begin to reinforce stereotypes of women and suggest character flaws or, worse, gender traits, and this characterization would defeat Modleski's intentions. This is a rhetorical *and* a methodological issue.

But these suggestions should not overwhelm the fundamental appreciation of an advance in the scholarship of this field of outstanding proportions. This book will be the measure of contributions in this field for some time to come. Its originality and clarity offer an inspirational model for scholars in film who want to apply new theoretical interest in psychology, consumption, and the audience to the experience of female viewers.

Quar. Rev. of Film & Video, Vol. 11, pp. 117–120
Reprints available directly from the publisher
Photocopying permitted by license only

Harwood Academic Publishers, 1989
Printed in the United States of America

Review Essay

Rosie the Riveter—Construction or Reflection?

Denise Mann

Maureen Honey. *Creating Rosie the Riveter: Class, Gender and Propaganda During World War II*. Amherst: University of Massachusetts Press, 1984. 251 pp. $20.00 cloth. $9.95 paper.

Creating Rosie the Riveter considers the effect of the romance between the state and the mass market magazine industry during WWII on the media's representations of women. As a result of wartime shortages, both the advertising and magazine industries were in jeopardy. By complying with government propaganda demands to recruit female labor into wartime production, these two otherwise expendable industries were able to secure their place in the reorganized, wartime marketplace. Chapter one of Maureen Honey's book provides a highly useful and informative account of the ways in which the media cooperated with the Office of War Information (OWI) and its various subsidiary agencies. In subsequent chapters, however, Honey subverts the provocative implications of this state/media interaction by narrowing her focus to analyses of thematic oppositions in the mass magazine at the level of content and story. By assuming that the media "reflects" its social context unproblematically, Honey loses sight of the larger ideological and institutional dynamics underlying her analysis of the mass media and their social construction of female roles.

The advertising and mass media industries served the state by molding public opinion to mobilize labor and sell war bonds and also by encouraging a renewed emphasis on consumerism in the postwar period of economic recovery. During the wartime labor crisis, magazine editors and advertisers served immediate state goals by constructing positive images of women in fields previously dominated by males. They secured the longer-range goal of retaining women as primary consumers for the home by designating these jobs as temporary deviations from women's "real" role as housewives. Advertisers' cooperation with government propaganda agencies should not be viewed as a gesture of self-sacrifice; instead, as Honey notes, advertiser involvement in the war bond sales and other issues related to the national emergency provided them with a means of keeping company names in women's minds despite restrictions on domestic production. Finally, by convincing women that their traditional role as primary consumer for the family was still operative, advertisers were laying the groundwork for the postwar resumption of consumerism as a way of life.

DENISE MANN is writing her doctoral dissertation on the star/product relation in early television programming at the University of California at Los Angeles, 90024. She is an associate editor of Camera Obscura.

These provocative discoveries about the advertising industry's intersection with government propaganda agencies should be seen as the historical context of the mass market magazine's representations of women in wartime America; however, in most cases Honey fails to integrate these findings into her analysis of texts. A methodological lapse is partly to blame: Honey uses content analyses of ads and fiction from *True Story* and *The Saturday Evening Post* to highlight the contradictory representations of women's wartime social roles—as wartime worker and housewife; but she has no means of accounting for reader resistance to and negotiation of this conflicting set of demands.

Honey's exploration of a historically specific audience, which is organized along class and gender lines, provides a valuable contribution to the study of the mass media, countering those studies which assume a monolithic "mass" audience. Despite the initial promise underlying her analyses of magazines aimed at "differentiated" audiences, Honey's emphasis on texts as "reflective" leads her to false conclusions. Honey's methodological model does not conceive of the mass media as popular constructions of common-sense solutions to problems incurred in a period of ideological crisis (such as wartime America). Instead, she sees these texts as reflections of predetermined social values serving primarily to reinforce traditional behavior in women.

The problem endemic to mass communications projects which use empiricist techniques is the tendency to isolate fixed categories in order to duplicate the classificatory divisions of scientific inquiry. In this case, Honey uses content analysis to chart the number of progressive vs. traditional representations of women in each magazine—looking for ways in which these images reflect or distort patterns in the "real" world. The confessional magazine industry, Honey tells us, did not respond to government wartime agencies' demand that the magazine produce positive images of women; in the confessional, characters did not tend to enter upwardly mobile, skilled, and executive-level jobs. Honey acknowledges that the confessional's failure to incorporate progressive images may in part have been due to economic restraints: their limited advertising revenue made them dependent on predictable formulas to keep costs low and insure reader loyalty. Ultimately, however, Honey concludes that confessional stories did not show women in upwardly mobile jobs because these positions were unavailable to working-class readers.[1]

Despite her interest in highly specified social groups, Honey doesn't provide responses of actual readers.[2] Nor does she theorize the implied systems of address inherent in these two media forms—the narratological and rhetorical strategies responsible for channeling readers' responses to their enunciative address along certain predictable lines. Instead, she derives a set of working hypotheses about the likely responses of readers to these two magazines based on her own biases and preconceptions about each social group. Rather than explicating the hierarchies imbedded in the mass media, Honey reproduces these social inequalities in her analysis by subscribing to a preexisting theory of class.

In singling out the representation of class in these two magazines, other discrepancies emerge. For instance, Honey chooses one magazine of each type to make claims about all slick and all confessional magazines. While *True Story* is aimed primarily at a female audience, the same can not be said of the general interest format of *The Saturday Evening Post.* Honey ignores this divergence in editorial policy in order to simplify the terms of her analysis. Despite the superficial elegance of her equation, the differences between the two magazines' institutional histories, production strategies, and use of formulaic as opposed to flexible, evolving editorial formats make Honey's goal of isolating class and gender problematic.

Briefly, the confessional magazine presented its stories in the first person, representing these fictions as "actual" accounts of "real" reader's lives. The discursive techniques of personal testimony and "eavesdropping" in the confessional would have produced a more insistent identification between the reader and the central character. As Honey points out, these first-person accounts of the tragic lives of individuals followed a "sin, suffer, and repent" formula. The contradictory status of the confessional as at once a "documented" event and as a "fictionalized construction" (writers duplicated the first-person "confessional" tone) suggests that the reader's relation to this text would have been complex and highly negotiated. By insisting that confessional readers responded only to those elements of the story which "reflected" their actual conditions, Honey mistakenly assumes that readers could not separate these highly formulaic, fictive worlds from their own lives.

In the first chapter of her book, "Creation of the Myth," Honey notes the disparity between the government's and industry's targeted audience of white, middle-class housewives and the actual status of most wartime workers: they were primarily students, married, widowed, or divorced working-class women of all ages who were dependent on these jobs for their economic survival. Honey's inability to account for these ideologically inflected "assumptions about women workers at the highest levels of government and industry" (p. 24)—their emphasis on the white, middle-class housewife—is related to her inability to account for the contradictions in the slick magazine's representation of women's social roles (idealized as the "Rosie the Riveter" factory worker *and* as the long-suffering wife and mother).

In her conclusion, Honey argues that sheer quantities of positive images of women made the *Post* a more "progressive" magazine then *True Story.* On the contrary, one could argue that the progressive images of white, middle-class housewives in wartime jobs in the *Post* were compatible with both the state's and the media's long-range ideological goals of having women return to the home after the war in order to "manage" consumption for the family. Furthermore, one could go on to argue that the slick magazine industry was better equipped than the confessional to "engineer" a reader's response along the lines which were conducive to the ebb and flow of the marketplace (based on its greater access to advertising revenue, and technical innovations such as color, elaborate layouts integrating editorial and advertising features, etc.). By isolating the numbers of progressive vs. nonprogressive images of women in the slick vs. the pulp magazine (pp. 188–189), Honey loses sight of how these multiple and dynamic mechanisms contribute to the production and reception of these images.

Any consideration of the mass market magazine must account for the process of mediation by which the media industry legitimizes existing systems of social stratification.[3] Honey's book outlines the complexity and scope of this project, providing numerous indications of directions for future work. However, by viewing the representations of the working class in *True Story* magazine as a product of that class's limited social mobility, Honey appears to have fallen prey to the same processes of ideological legitimation of social inequality which she has set out to uncover.

NOTES

1. Honey, p. 202: "One, more convincing reason for the failure of *True Story* to feature women in authoritative, nontraditional roles is that its readers were extremely unlikely to find managerial or professional positions in the real world."
2. Honey, pp. 171–172. Honey uses interviews with former aircraft workers as evidence that the fictionalized accounts of women wartime workers were accurate reflections of working-class women's positive experiences. The slide that has occurred is one in which actual readers' responses to the popular literature have been replaced by women without any connection to the magazines—thereby cutting across the fiction/reality split and ignoring the complex processes of identification and resistance that go into the reading activity.
3. Graham Murdock and Peter Golding, "Capitalism, Communication and Class Relations," in *Mass Communication and Society*, ed. J. Curran, M. Gurevitch, and J. Woolacott (London: Edward Arnold, 1979), p. 39. Murdock and Golding note that "radical inequalities in the distribution of rewards have come to be represented as natural and inevitable. . . ."

Quar. Rev. of Film & Video, Vol. 11, pp. 121–125
Reprints available directly from the publisher
Photocopying permitted by license only

Harwood Academic Publishers, 1989
Printed in the United States of America

Review Essay

Mass Images of Consumption

Giuliana Muscio

Stuart Ewen and Elizabeth Ewen. *The Channels of Desire: Mass Images and the Shaping of American Consciousness*. New York: McGraw-Hill, 1982. 312 pp. $12.95 cloth. $7.95 paper.

Judith Williamson. *Decoding Advertisements: Ideology and Meaning in Advertising*. New York: M. Boyars, 1978. 180 pp. $8.95 paper.

It is widely understood that women play the predominant role in the culture of consumerism: they are the target audience for the complex ensemble of the image-making media. *Channels of Desire* and *Decoding Advertisements* represent two attempts to offer a critical understanding of consumer culture and of the role of women in the ideological configurations that sustain it. These books also share some convictions: one methodological—that such studies are necessarily interdisciplinary—the other historiographic and political—that explaining the functioning of the media and unraveling the production of a false consciousness is in itself a valuable radical gesture.

The basic assumption from which Stuart and Elizabeth Ewen start their analytical study of consumer culture in America is that American capitalism is characterized by "the ability to erect a unity of opposites, social and economic disparity along with a mask of parity" (p. 177). Thus their work is structured within a binary system, which articulates the economic-technological developments with their sociocultural effects, in a continuous series of chain reactions. In this model, one phase of the development of capitalist economy induces a change in the technology of production, which affects social life and interacts with the culture of the audience-consumer. The Ewens focus their attention on media and mediation. They analyze a system which includes not only traditional mass media, but also fashion, design, and other popular arts. "The mass media and the industries of fashion and design, through the production and distribution of imagery, have reconciled widespread vernacular demands for a better life with the general priorities of corporate capitalism" (p. 37).

At the beginning there was the machine. The machine produced "wage slavery," but also the new means for reproducing things usually limited to upper classes. For example, mid-15th century printing developed out of the needs of commerce and introduced the first mechanical mass production, "the prototype for the machine

GIULIANA MUSCIO, while completing a doctoral dissertation at UCLA on the relationship between Hollywood and the New Deal, teaches film history and criticism at the University of Padua in Italy and is the author of three books and articles on blacklisting and government/film industry relations.

age." But printing also allowed for a more democratic dissemination of information and knowledge, "central in the unraveling of old, feudal seats of authority and power." The Ewens see a similar pattern in the history of movies and fashion. In 1915 *Scientific American* described the motion picture camera as a device for creating illusionistic entertainment and escape,[1] and as a means for conducting time-motion studies of industrial workers. Later, in the nickelodeon stage, the movies both educated the masses of immigrant workers, "americanizing" them, and satisfied their need for communal experience, adapting their customary world view— mostly rural and nonindustrial—to the facts of city living. After World War I, through the star system, the movies articulated a new model of feminine behavior, by way of the vamp and Mary Pickford's interpretation of the gamine, speaking to the new "sexual dynamics" of an American society in which the disruption of the patriarchal family had given women and younger people space to develop new roles. But the star system—as the site of work—also produced a kind of "slavery" in the contractual limitations imposed on these performers.

Whereas *Captains of Consciousness* presents the interaction between the economic-technological base and the sociocultural superstructure in the mechanically deterministic way, and is also flawed by the application of inadequate "conspiracy theories," in *Channels of Desire* hegemony is not so much imposed on a mass of passive consumers as it is interactive with their *mentality*. Even if the Ewens do not refer to the Gramscian concept of common sense[2] and do not use the term "mentality" with the connotations that "nouvelle histoire" has given it,[3] their approach implies both. The most interesting contribution of the book is constituted precisely by the analysis of the impact of the new images of a mass-producing, mass-consuming society on "vernacular demands," "customary bonds," and "traditional culture."

As Stuart Ewen has articulated in *Captains of Consciousness*, the machine age transformed the home from the place of production into the place of consumption, radically changing the role of the patriarchal family, and therefore the position of women in it, electing them as the *managers* of consumption. Within this development, through which capitalistic economy ensures mass production through the ideology of consumerism, the textile and fashion industries are more than a section in the economic and technological history of the American industry. They are in fact advanced and crucial elements of this development. They are parallel to printing in their image-making and social control functions. "For capitalism, mechanical production and image-making have long shared the same quilt" (p. 16). For the Ewens, fashion constitutes a singular domain of capitalistic economy. For example, in Victorian times, the complexity and weight of women's clothes restricted movement. Corsets provoked breathing problems and fainting, which originated the image of the fragile Victorian virgin. The "S-curve" silhouette, shaped by corsets and bustles, and the absence of underpants (considered as demi-mondaines' garments) implied in these women a "sexual readiness" which contradicted the careful and modest wrapping of the entire body, the negation of sexual availability. "Within the framework of dress restraint, women combined the reciprocal categories of purity and sin" (p. 142). "Clothing tended to consolidate the female body into bountiful masses, weighty and ponderous symbols of success" (p. 148).

The Ewens depict a large fresco of urban life, with department stores, billboards, windows, and mirrors for the mesmerized consumers, a world of colors and shapes, of haunting images, from labels to chromolithographs, from screens to Sears catalogs, from paper dolls to newspaper ads—a world of images which at the same time stimulates consumption and enriches the perceptual-sensorial experience of the consumer-spectator.

The consumer the Ewens describe is identified with a sociopsychological idea of the "self," in which emotional needs and noncognitive and sensorial elements predominate. "*The self* becomes the haunted repository of sensitivity, vulnerability and emotion, of need and desire. The *commodity* increasingly invades the realm of satisfaction" (p. 262).

"The world view of chaos—as projected by the media array—is intrinsically narcissistic, not in the sense that it talks about the self, but that it re-enacts the shattered experience of the self on the level of a spectacle, a spectacle to be consumed" (p. 269). This perceptual fragmentation of experience within mass consumer culture is deliberately replicated by the Ewens in the structure of the book itself, with its montages of written oral history and nonlinear and nonchronological—at times confusing—narrative.

The Ewens appear to hold a pessimistic view of the subject as an irrational entity,[4] fully determined by economic and cultural production.[5] This definition of the subject is correlated with the overall interpretation of the media system as a series of chain reactions. In this binary system, the dialectical dynamism is truncated, depriving it of a potential political articulation. Mechanical oppositions or cause-effect sequences do not allow for intervention. Ideological criticism—as is often the case in American radical writing—is trapped in utopian projects, in transcendental solutions, short of political programs. "To establish popular initiative, consumerism must be transcended" (p. 77). Transcendence appears to be the only possible answer to an interpretation of the contemporary world as being "out of control and out of reach." Reifying the *chain*, in the system of mediation,[6] the Ewens can only propose countercultural uses of that system. "Beyond continual political analysis, it is necessary to challenge that dominion" (p. 281). "The spectacle must be acted upon, collectively" (p. 282). It is a disappointing conclusion to such a stimulating work on the development of the media in American culture.

Decoding Advertisements takes up a position within the same terrain, namely the articulation of self/society as mediated by consumer imagery. This book is mainly composed of a series of textual analyses of ads. It is like an anthology of advertisements, which includes pictures and a detailed examination of "advertisement work." The individual chapters are constructed as theoretical frameworks for the specific analyses. Structurally the book is divided into two parts, "Advertising Work" and "Referent Systems." Chapter 1 deals with the ad as "transference of meaning," describing the process by which an object "replaces" or "stands for" an image or feeling; then the product "replaces" the original object in this role, and appropriates the meaning of that image or feeling (p. 40). Subsequently, "the subject that makes the exchange" is examined, that is, "the subject as reproduced by the ad . . . What the advertisement clearly does is thus to signify, to represent to us, the *object* of desire. Since that object *is the self*, this means that, while ensnaring/creating the subject through his or her exchange of signs, the advertisement is actually feeding off that subject's desire for coherence and meaning in him or in her self" (p. 60). Chapter 3 deals with "the world as world of signs to be deciphered," or, as Williamson writes: "In the process of deciphering *signs*, we are constituted as the discoverers of meaning, and are involved in a 'conscious' activity which keeps us looking through a certain opacity in the signifying process, to a message beyond; thus although involved in a hermeneutic and limited 'deciphering' we overlook the signifying process itself" (p. 73). Part II, devoted to the referent systems, discusses "Cooking Nature" and "Back to Nature"—that is, the relationship nature/culture and the processes of reification accomplished by the "advertisement work," "Magic" ("a mythical means of doing things"), and "Time: Narrative and History." In this chapter, Williamson argues: "Thus time is given a 'being' rather than a material existence: the synchronicity must be outside real time, since all time is available to us at once as we stand in real time, in front of the ad" (p. 155).

At times amusing, at times revelatory, the textual analyses of ads in *Decoding Advertisements* are pleasant to read. As in *Channels of Desire*, with its history of blue jeans or of the department store, explanations of pieces of everyday life impose themselves as stunning revelations, precisely because of their application and to taken-for-granted presences in the world of objects that have been alienated and reified in such a way that they have lost their characters as cultural artifacts.

Decoding Advertisements was written in 1978, and reprinted in 1981 and 1983, with a new preface. But, it is not one of those books which "ages" well. On the contrary, its simplistic structuralist-semiotic approach appears dated, and therefore its utility as a "cultural handbook" has waned. The theoretical framework within which Judith Williamson has proposed her "decoding" of ads belongs to that kind of intellectual bricolage that makes "systematists" and theoreticians jump from their seats. "I am impatient," she writes "with any theory of ideology which is not tied to anything practical, to the material factors which influence our feelings, our lives, our images of ourselves . . . [But] I have used other people's ideas as tools: I have taken the tools which have been useful in 'decoding' advertisements and rejected the others. This is not being 'eclectic' but being practical" (p. 10). Even if we can find some of these statements in the introduction charming, in their desire to solve their unresolvable asystematicity in the revolutionary impetus of the enterprise and in their pragmatic tone, they do make it difficult to accept and use this book again today.

Quotes from sacred texts abound, appearing at the beginning of each chapter as an invocation for cultural protection or as an illuminating commandment coming from a superior knowledge. Therefore Marx, Freud, Saussure, Lacan, Althusser, Lévi-Strauss, Peirce stand before the analysis of the ad for Chanel no. 5 or for a cigarette brand—which is, in itself, absolutely appropriate, because a semiotic study of advertisements is as legitimate as a semiotic analysis of Proust. Besides, it is particularly appropriate to Williamson's strategy and desire to bridge the gap between a complex theoretical body of knowledges and the need for its concrete application. In the "Preface to the Fourth Impression," she argues: "But the increasing bulk of stuff that gets written in academic journals and so on means that the distance is ever widening between those whose careers *depend* on honing down theories finer and finer, and those 'non-specialists' who come across, and need, the structural-semiotic approach as part of a way of seeing society in general. It would be more radical at present to try to close the gap, not widen it." One can sympathize with this effort, but still *Decoding Advertisements* does not go beyond proposing "critical understanding" and the reappropriation of the "work of advertisements."

"The need for relationship and human meaning appropriated by advertising is one that, if only it was not diverted, could radically change the society we live in" (p. 14). But the decoding of "advertisement work," which is somewhat analogous to Freud's "dream work" in Williamson's definition, is not as "liberatory" and does not affect consciousness as the interpretation of a dream would. The problem of false consciousness is not resolved by acts of revelation or self-analysis.

It is in the nature of the semiotic work to deal with the production of meaning and not with the production of the cultural objects examined. Still, the task—as Williamson anticipates—is not just "to criticize advertisements on the ground of dishonesty and exploitation," but to explain their ideological function. But is the description of a process equivalent to its explanation? And would "explanation" be enough to change the advertisement work and the system which sustains it?

In both books, psychological and psychoanalytical concerns seem to confuse the definition of consciousness more than help it. This common trait seems to indicate a dangerous inclination to identify the subject—here, women consumers—as psychological entities, attributing to them fears, needs, and desire, but not a mind. On one side, this attitude represents a trace of the traditional prejudice which identifies women with emotionality; on the other side, perhaps, it points to a self-constructed trap in women's studies, that is, the reification of disciplinary tools—such as psychoanalysis—into thematic concerns.

Besides, the faith in the critical act obscures the need for political action and real social change, proposing "transcendental" or "countercultural" intellectual escapes.

NOTES

1. "Appropriating, to some extent, the language of the unconscious, of dream and of myth in its imagery, the movie camera could dissociate itself from the tedium of the mechanical process, and realign itself with those realms of existence repressed by the harsh rationalism of 'world-machine' ideology" (*The Channels of Desire*, p. 35).

2. Gramsci defined common sense as "the philosophy of the non-philosophers," which "contains elements of the Stone Age and principles of a more advanced science, prejudices from all past phases of history at the local level and intuitions of a future philosophy, which will be that of the human race united the world over" (quoted in *Gramsci and Marxist Theory*, ed. Chantal Mouffe [London: Routledge & Kegan Paul, 1979], p. 17).

3. Most of all in Georges Duby's work and in particular in "Histoire sociale et idéologies des les sociétés," in *Faire Histoire* (Paris: Gallimard, 1974), or in Jacques LeGoff, "Histoire de la mentalité," in *Nouvelle Histoire* (Paris: Gallimard, 1979).

4. The Ewens pay a ritual tribute to the work of Warren Susman on the definition of the self within American culture of the 20th century, but they do not take into account its implications. Susman's concepts of "personality" and "character," developed in relation to the changing culture of consumer society, seem to me better equipped than the Ewens' to discuss cultural history and to create a space for change in society (Warren Susman, *Culture as History* [New York: Pantheon, 1984]).

5. "If Frankenstein provides us with a telling metaphor for a technological world out of reach and out of control, it is the development of communication systems, to a large extent, that has placed the world beyond the network of popular discourse" (*The Channels of Desire*, p. 27).

6. "On a narrow economic level, the origin of mass culture can be seen as an extension of the necessity to generate and maintain an industrial labor force and expand markets. Yet both of these imperatives were inextricably linked to cultural and perceptual processes of change" (*The Channels of Desire*, p. 57).

Notes for Contributors

Typescripts

Submissions: Papers should be typed with double spacing and wide (3 cm) margins, using one side of the paper only, and submitted in triplicate to the editorial office: **Quarterly Review of Film and Video, School of Cinema-Television, University of Southern California, Division of Critical Studies, Los Angeles, California 90089-2211.** Papers are accepted only in English. Manuscripts do not receive further copyediting by the publisher or typesetter; authors should ensure before submission that papers are correct in style and language.

Author affiliations: Authors should include a blurb of one or two sentences providing a complete mailing address and a brief description of research interests and publications.

Acknowledgments: Include acknowledgments in the "Notes" section at the end of the paper.

Terms of acceptance: Submission of a manuscript is taken to imply that the paper represents original work not previously published, is not being considered elsewhere for publication, and if accepted for publication, will not be published elsewhere in the same form, in any language, without the consent of the publisher. It is also assumed that the author has obtained all necessary permissions to include in the paper items such as quotations, reprinted figures, results of government-sponsored research, etc. It is a condition of acceptance for publication that the publisher acquires copyright of the paper throughout the world.

Figures

All figures should be numbered with consecutive arabic numerals, have descriptive captions, and be mentioned in the text. Figures should be supplied with the manuscript, but kept separate. Indicate position for each figure in the margin. A list of figure captions, with relevant figure numbers, should be typed on a separate sheet and included with the typescript. Capitalize only the first letter of the first word in the figure captions.

All figures must be of a high enough standard for direct reproduction. Line drawings should be prepared in black ink on white paper, with all labels, lettering, and symbols included. Photographs must be black-and-white glossy prints of good quality. Using a pencil, clearly label each figure with the author's name and figure number; indicate top where this is not obvious. Figures should be submitted as close to final size as possible to minimize reduction. Figures will be sized to fit a column width of about 12.5 cm. Redrawing or retouching of unusable figures will be charged to authors.

Tables

Tables should be typed on separate sheets, numbered consecutively with roman numerals, and have a short descriptive caption at the top. Capitalize the first letter of the first word in table captions. Tables may be placed in the typescript immediately following the page of text with which they should be printed, or they may be grouped separately. In the latter case, indicate in the text where the tables are to appear. Avoid the use of vertical rules in tables. Each table should be mentioned in the text.

References

References follow the form used in *The Chicago Manual of Style*. All notes should be collected at the end of the paper under the heading "Notes" and not at the bottom of individual pages. Examples:

1. Charles Eckert, "The Carole Lombard in Macy's Window," *Quarterly Reivew of Film Studies* 3, no. 1 (Winter 1978): 4.
2. David Bordwell, Janet Staiger, and Kristin Thompson, *The Classical Hollywood Cinema: Film Style and Mode of Production to 1960* (New York: Columbia University Press, 1985), pp. 19–21.
3. Carl Laemmle, "The Business of Motion Pictures," in *The American Film Industry*, ed. Tino Balio (Madison: University of Wisconsin Press, 1976), p. 163.

Text Headings

Type first-level headings in capital letters over to the left; begin the text on the following line. Second-level headings should be typed in lowercase letters but with all main words capitalized; begin the text on the following line. For third-level headings, only the first letter should be a capital; underline, then run on the text after three spaces.

Proofs and Reprints

Authors will receive page proofs (including figures) by airmail. Corrected proofs must be returned to the address indicated within two days. Authors' alterations in excess of 10% of the original composition cost will be charged to authors. There are no publication page charges to individuals or institutions. Reprints may be ordered by completing the appropriate form sent with proofs.